W9-BNB-452

TRENDS VERY BEST
Kitchens & Bathrooms

Time Inc. Home Entertainment
Publisher: Richard Fraiman
Executive Director, Marketing Services: Carol Pittard
Director, Retail & Special Sales: Tom Mifsud
Marketing Director, Branded Businesses: Swati Rao
Director, New Product Development: Peter Harper
Financial Director: Steven Sandonato
Assistant General Counsel: Dasha Smith Dwin
Prepress Manager: Emily Rabin
Book Production Manager: Suzanne Janso
Product Manager: Victoria Alfonso
Associate Prepress Manager: Anne-Michelle Gallero

Special thanks to Bozena Bannett, Glenn Buonocore, Robert
Marasco, Brooke McGuire, Jonathan Polsky, Chavaughn
Raines, Ilene Schreider, Adriana Tierno, Britney Williams

Published by
Time Inc. Home Entertainment
Time Inc.
1271 Avenue of the Americas
New York, New York 10020

ISBN: 1-933405-10-4

Time Inc. Home Entertainment is a trademark of Time Inc.

Trends Publishing International
Publisher: David Johnson
Managing Director: Adam Hasselberg
President: Judy Johnson
Editorial Director: Paul Taylor
Managing Editor: John Williams
Sales Manager: Craig Williams
Art Direction: Sarah Melrose
Design: Annalise Ryan
Production Director: Louise Messer
Production Manager: Brent Carville

TRENDS VERY BEST KITCHENS AND BATHROOMS.
Copyright © 2006 by Trends Publishing USA Inc. All rights
reserved. Printed in the United States of America. No part
of this book may be used or reproduced in any manner
whatsoever without written permission. For information
or more copies contact Trends Publishing USA Inc.,
49 Main Highway, Ellerslie, Auckland, New Zealand or
Time Inc. Home Entertainment, 1271 Avenue of the
Americas, New York, New York 10020.

For more great kitchen and bathroom ideas visit
www.Trendsideas.com

Contents

Introduction   **4**

Kitchens   **6**

Traditional kitchens   8

Hub of the home   34

Contemporary design   54

For the serious cook   80

Bathrooms   **104**

Bathtubs as centerpieces   106

Master suites   122

Links to the outdoors   148

Colors & materials   168

Index   **190**

For more great kitchen and bathroom ideas
visit **www.trendsideas.com**

Introduction

Your kitchen and bathroom are the two hardest working areas of the home. But long gone are the days when they were considered merely an efficient arrangement of work surfaces, and a collection of fixtures and fittings – a place to prepare meals and clean up after, or somewhere to bathe at the start and end of each day.

Today's kitchens and bathrooms are created as living areas, where homeowners can spend as much time relaxing and enjoying the ambiance as doing chores.

The driving force behind this change comes from our increasing desire make best use of space in our homes by taking a more open approach. So the walls have been coming down to create larger, connected areas rather than boxed-off rooms.

This trend has been most apparent in the main living area, where the kitchen has been opened up to the dining room and informal lounge to produce the Great Room. No longer is the person who is preparing the meal cut off from other family members or guests.

We're also seeing the same trend to open up happening with the bathroom – particularly the master bath, with its connections to other areas in the master suite.

As our tastes change, designers are taking a new perspective on kitchens and bathrooms. If they are part of a living space, they need to be designed as living spaces. We need to think of their components as furniture rather than storage cabinets. And we need to carefully consider how they relate to the adjacent areas.

In this first edition of Trends Very Best Kitchens and Bathrooms, we showcase how leading architects and designers have approached the changing dynamics of these two key rooms. Each of the featured projects has been selected for its practical and aesthetic solutions to the challenges the homeowner and designer faced.

These case studies will supply the inspiration and ideas you need to design your new kitchen and bathroom – which in turn can help bring about radical changes to your lifestyle and well-being.

Paul Taylor
Editorial Director
Trends

Kitchens

The hub of the home – it may have become a bit of a cliché, but it's a still a phrase that neatly sums up the status of today's kitchen. The kitchen is the central focus for activity first thing in the morning and in the early evening – and, in many households, regularly through the rest of the day, too. It's the place the family head to when they first get home from school or work, and then return to for snacks while watching TV or entertaining friends.

As a result, the kitchen has transformed from a closed-off workspace at the back of the living areas to a centrally located showpiece, designed to integrate with adjacent spaces in the home.

When you start out designing a new kitchen, there are three strands to the decision-making:

- what do you want your kitchen to look like?
- what's the most efficient and ergonomic arrangement of the component parts within the space you've got?
- what will it cost?

Take a look at this

It's easy to dismiss aesthetics as just the window-dressing on a design. But in reality most of us have a look or a style that we're going to feel comfortable with. So this is probably the easiest aspect to clear up right from the start.

Go through all the kitchens in this section and note those you like the look of. While we might like to think that our new kitchen is going to be unique, it's probably going to fall into one of three main style categories – traditional, transitional or contemporary. While there's still a lot of variation within these categories, you need to establish which one appeals to you the most.

Don't limit yourself to a kitchen that's exactly what you want. If you like traditional style, look at all the traditional kitchens and pick out what aspect of each one you like. It may just be a color in one case, or a faucet design in another.

It's even an advantage to check out kitchens you don't like. You may still find something that appeals to you, no matter how small a part it may play in your final design.

If you take this approach, we guarantee it will be a great help and time-saver for whoever puts together your final design.

Down to practicalities

There are many specialist aspects to consider when working on the space planning and organization of appliances and other fittings in a kitchen.

If you want to avoid costly mistakes or inefficient layouts, it definitely pays to get an expert to help you with your final design. You can play an active role in this stage by reading how homeowners and designers of our featured kitchens worked through the design process together.

Be prepared to listen to what your kitchen designer advises, even if at first it doesn't seem to be exactly what you want. A good designer will draw on their expertise and experience to give you more than you thought possible.

Remember that the kitchen you design now may need to last up to 10 years … possibly longer. When you add in the cost of all the components, this is one of the most expensive rooms in your home. So you want as much future-proofing as you can get.

Counting the cost

How much will my new kitchen cost? How long's a piece of string?

Really, this is the wrong question, because there's no precise answer.

The question you should be asking yourself is 'How much do I have in my budget?', since the price of a kitchen can vary tremendously. You can design a kitchen for as little as $10,000, or pay in excess of $200,000.

One factor that determines the cost is size. The bigger the kitchen, the more you put into it, the more it costs.

If you're renovating a kitchen, and the old space wasn't big enough, you'll need to budget for construction costs to increase the available size, either with an addition to the house or by extending the kitchen into an adjacent area. But be warned – many homeowners start down this track and, before they know it, the project has suddenly transformed to a full-scale remodel of the whole house!

The materials you use and the brand of appliances you choose will also dramatically affect the final cost of your new kitchen.

As you look through the various kitchen projects in this book, you should also identify the appliances, materials and fittings you like. Put them on your wish list and note what you like about each one. A quick search on the internet will usually tell you whether a particular item on your list is within your budget range.

Have all this information on hand when you talk to a designer, who should be able to suggest alternatives that best meet your requirements and budget.

Time to start

You're at the beginning of an exciting process. The ideas and inspiration you encounter on the following pages will help equip you for what should turn out to be an enjoyable and rewarding process.

1

Traditional kitchens

"Large or small, new or remodeled, there's nothing more homey than a well-crafted, traditional-style kitchen."

Craig Dixon, designer, Todd Pritchett Design Studio

Heart and soul

Positioned in the middle of the house, this kitchen is the center of daily life for a busy family

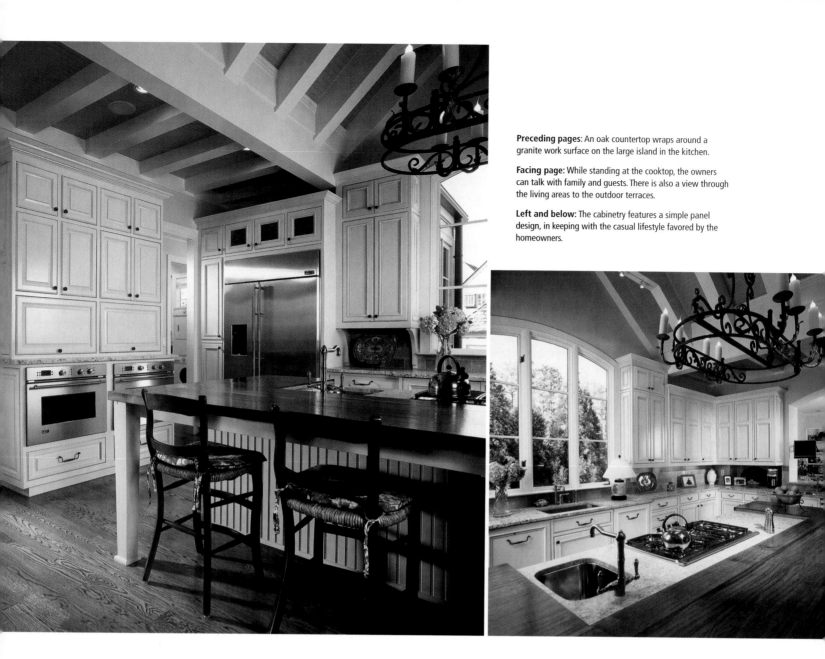

Preceding pages: An oak countertop wraps around a granite work surface on the large island in the kitchen.

Facing page: While standing at the cooktop, the owners can talk with family and guests. There is also a view through the living areas to the outdoor terraces.

Left and below: The cabinetry features a simple panel design, in keeping with the casual lifestyle favored by the homeowners.

For many people, the most appealing aspect of a home is the casual, relaxed lifestyle that goes with it. The comfortable decor, the easy flow between rooms and the seamless transition to the outdoors all contribute to the enjoyment.

It's a way of living that the owners of this new house wanted to hold on to, say designers Todd Pritchett and Craig Dixon.

"The family has a mountain lake house, which we also designed," says Pritchett. "It provides a very casual living environment, and the owners wanted their new Atlanta house to incorporate some of the elements that make for such an easy lifestyle – but with a little more sophistication."

A central kitchen was crucial to the design, Dixon says. As the owners like to entertain and have several children, the kitchen is the center of activity.

"Everything flows to the kitchen. It was always going to be a very social space, so we fully integrated it into the architecture of the house. The floor plan is a modern layout with light-filled spaces, but detailed with the understated elegance of a historic home."

Painted and glazed cabinetry that complements the wood detailing elsewhere in the house helps to visually link the kitchen with the adjacent rooms. These include a breakfast room and a family room, which leads out to a courtyard and swimming pool. In addition, the kitchen opens to a walk-in butler's pantry, formal dining room, home office and laundry room.

With so many openings, designing the work space wasn't straightforward, says Pritchett.

"Trying to get the traffic to flow through the space, yet still provide for plenty of storage, was challenging," he says. "The large size of the kitchen also posed problems in respect to scale."

This page: The countertop closest to the breakfast room functions as a beverage center. It incorporates a sink, and has an undercounter refrigerator.

Facing page: This new kitchen is open to the main family living areas, including the breakfast room.

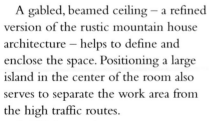

A gabled, beamed ceiling – a refined version of the rustic mountain house architecture – helps to define and enclose the space. Positioning a large island in the center of the room also serves to separate the work area from the high traffic routes.

A 12ft-long oak countertop wraps around a granite surface on the island. When viewed from the family room the island resembles a country table, – another link with the vacation home.

"Using a combination of materials and levels for the countertop helps to break up the mass, so the island is not so overwhelming," says Dixon.

Despite the size of the kitchen, the work triangle is compact, due to the close proximity of the main sink, the cooktop and refrigerator. Twin ovens are also close by, built into an appliance pantry. Lifting pocket doors above the ovens slide away to expose a microwave oven and coffee machine.

Dixon says the kitchen is designed so more than one person at a time can work at the countertops. There are two additional sinks – one beside the cooktop, and one on a counter that also serves as a beverage center.

Architecture and kitchen design: Todd Pritchett and Craig Dixon, Todd Pritchett Design Studio (Atlanta, GA)

Interior designer: Anne Lippincott Interiors

Flooring: Wide plank oak

Custom cabinetry: Painted and light-glazed maple from Skyline Design Group

Countertops: Bianco Romero granite and French oak

Backsplash: French limestone by Walker Zanger

Sinks: Blanco

Faucets: Rohl

Ovens and refrigerator: GE Monogram

Ventilation and cooktop: Thermador

Dishwasher: Bosch

Undercounter refrigerator and icemaker: U-Line

Photography by John Umberger

A sense of connection

With its large openings to family living and dining areas, this kitchen is the social hub of the house

Left: This kitchen in a new house links with both the formal dining room and a family living area – all part of one large open-plan space.

Below: Large arches and columns help to visually separate the kitchen from the family living room, while still maintaining an openness. The openings also allow a view from the kitchen to the outdoor living area and pool beyond the French doors.

Even with the best intentions, home remodeling projects aren't always feasible. In extreme cases, it can be necessary to simply start over from scratch, as the owners of this home found.

But rebuilding a house also brings many benefits, including the chance to plan a kitchen to meet every requirement. For this young family, that meant a kitchen that would be the center of family activity – a space that would relate to the family living area and the formal dining room.

The owners commissioned architect Rick Lundin of 3 Studios, and interior designer Renee Hallberg of William Beson Interior Design to create an interior that would combine traditional old-world character with modern convenience.

"The house needed to cater to a modern lifestyle, and allow family members to interact with one another," says Lundin. "The design of the kitchen, in particular, needed to engage the family area, while still preserving the sense of a separate room."

To this end, the kitchen forms part of a large space devoted to family living and dining. Positioned on a south-facing wall, it receives morning sunlight and remains bright throughout the day. Large, curved arches and columns – a feature repeated elsewhere in the house – open the kitchen to the family living room.

"In contemporary homes there is often less definition between these two areas. Here, the arches and columns help define the kitchen space, while still providing a sense of openness," says Lundin. "The design also allows family members and guests to converse,

Below: The old-world character is enhanced by a butler's sink, an iron chandelier and the relatively simple detailing of the cabinetry.

Right: The traditional character of the house is reinforced in the kitchen accessories and detailing.

Facing page: A cooking center with a customized hood and decorative tiled backsplash, is the focal point of the kitchen. The cooker is in line with the island and the doors leading to the dining room.

without guests actually having to be in the kitchen."

Wide glass doors allow the kitchen to open up to the formal dining room on the other side. So, even with the doors closed, there is still a sense of connection.

The old-world character of the rest of the house continues in the kitchen, which is large enough to cater for several people working at once.

"The owners really like the dark wood and dark wall colors seen in traditional homesteads," says Hallberg. "We have continued the dark walnut floors through the kitchen, but there needed to be a balance so the kitchen wouldn't look too cavernous. For this reason the main cabinets are painted cream and ivory."

To create a visual link with the family room, the island base is painted in a blue-green hue. This is a slightly darker shade of the wall color used in the family room.

A cooking center at one end of the kitchen serves as the focal point of the room. It is in a direct line from the dining room, on the same axis as the island.

Additional cooking facilities are provided at the opposite end of the room.

"In a house of this size, there is an expectation the kitchen will be well suited to entertaining," says Lundin. "Therefore, providing large appliances and plenty of counter space is essential."

Ample storage was also a requirement. As well as the cabinet space, there are large wicker baskets for storing pots and pans.

Other accessories in keeping with the old-world character include an iron chandelier and traditionally styled faucets.

Architect: Richard C Lundin, AIA, 3 Studios (Minneapolis, MN)

Interior designer: Renee LeJeune Hallberg, Allied ASID, William Beson Interior Design

Cabinets: Painted birch wood

Countertops: Giallo Beach granite from Midwest Tile, Marble and Granite Inc; butcher's block

Flooring: Walnut from Excel Homes

Backsplash: Tiles from Tile by Design

Windows: Andersen

Paints: Benjamin Moore

Lighting: Chandelier from Renaissance Guild

Sink: Kohler

Faucets: Grohe

Wall oven, microwave, range, dishwasher and warming drawer: Viking

Ventilation: Vent-A-Hood

Refrigerator: Sub-Zero

Photography by John Umberger

Rich palette

A mix of finishes, soft warm colors, and previously owned
pieces add life and personality to this kitchen

Left: This kitchen has been designed for an active family life. The owner wanted her children to be able to come home and do homework at the breakfast bar while she cooks the dinner. A custom-made dining table in the same area is used for family meals. Several preparation areas mean snacks can be made, and meals cooked, without family members getting in each other's way.

Below: A built-in desk provides a convenient corner where the owner can do her own paperwork.

Faced with designing a kitchen for a new home, it's helpful to have some kind of starting point. You may prefer dark cabinetry because the room is flooded with sun all day long, or light colors because the space is small.

For the owner of this kitchen, a bolt of fabric was the inspiration. Judi Coté had a favorite floral fabric, which she wanted to use for the curtains.

"I've always loved strong colors and this fabric is a rich mixture – everything in the kitchen revolves round it," she says.

Cabinetry is in a creamy buttery tone, the island is stained brown to look old and beaten up, and the walls are pumpkin. All these tones are drawn from the colors within the curtains.

"I also wanted a traditional, wide-open kitchen that would work well for children, dogs and our busy family life," she says.

Two special pieces – an old Smallbone storage cabinet that the family has owned for about 10 years and the chandelier hanging over the dining table – keep past happy memories in the kitchen.

Below: The colors in the curtains above the French doors were inspiration for the kitchen's design.

Facing page: Turned legs on the breakfast bar, beaded paneling on cabinetry and a mix of materials all complement the country flavor of this kitchen.

Kitchen designer Shirley McFarlane says the kitchen was laid out to include these pieces. However, the ceiling, which slopes steeply up to a second-level balcony, also affected the design.

"Judi wanted the ovens and warming drawers on either side of the cooktop in a large hearth area, because it suited the way she planned to use the kitchen.

"However, with a steeply sloping ceiling above it, the hearth needed to be anchored in the kitchen, so it didn't look lost. We did this by taking the mantelpiece up to the height of the balcony," says the designer.

To give the kitchen a traditional look, the cabinet doors have beaded central panels, and the design incorporates several items made to look like pieces of furniture.

A freestanding cabinet at one end of the island has a checkerboard-patterned top that was custom made by a local artist. So the children join in with the cooking, this countertop is at a slightly lower level than the top on the main part of the island.

The breakfast bar on the back of the island seats four. It is higher than the food preparation section of the island, and with turned legs, it too looks like furniture.

To ensure this large kitchen is functional, one corner has been designated as a special area for the children's use. It includes a secondary sink in the countertop, an appliance garage for a toaster and kettle, a coffee machine, the refrigerator and microwave. There's also a television on a pull-out swivel.

Architect: David Grace, Classical Studio

Kitchen design: Shirley McFarlane, CKD (Atlanta, GA)

Interior designer: Judi Coté, European Habitat

Kitchen manufacturer: Acorn Kitchens

Fabrics: Gillian WF103-02 from The Winhall Collection

Cabinets, island, island table: Maple

Countertops: Verde Fontaine granite

Island top: Wenge and maple checkerboard made by Craft Art

Flooring: Brocarro tile from Traditions in Tile

Tiling: Ann Sacks (behind cooktop); Blatka Paneva tile (backsplash)

Stools and kitchen chairs: French country made by Antique Designs

Kitchen table: Serif glass and iron table from Kolkka Tables

Lighting: C Lighting

Chandelier: Studio Steel

Faucets: Rohl

Oven, cooktop, microwave, warming drawer: Thermador

Ventilation: Vent-A-Hood

Refrigerator: Sub-Zero

Dishwasher: Bosch

Photography by John Umberger

Left: A separate unit at one end of the island has a wenge and maple checkerboard countertop. The height difference makes it more accessible for the children's use. In a separate preparation area, in one corner of the kitchen, snacks can be put together. To add interest and reinforce the country look of the kitchen, the cupboards above the sink have chicken wire panels in the doors.

Old-world magic

This French country kitchen is characterized by strong attention to detail and a high level of craftsmanship

Architect: Zampolin & Associates
Kitchen designer: Amir J Lin (Paramus, NJ)
Interior designer: Barbara Ostrom
Kitchen manufacturer:
Küche+Cucina Handcrafted Cabinetry
Cabinets: Cherry, maple, mahogany; painted cabinetry
Flooring: Jerusalem Gold stone
Sink: Franke; Herbeau fireclay farmhouse apron sink
Faucets: Rohl
Oven: Viking
Ventilation: Custom stone hood from Küche+Cucina
Refrigerator: Sub-Zero
Dishwasher: KitchenAid

While we might have a very definite idea of the style of kitchen we want, it is always advantageous to bring in an expert.

The owners of this kitchen knew that they wanted a French country design that would incorporate mainly freestanding cabinetry. They invited Amir Ilin of Küche+Cucina to create their vision, in conjunction with interior designer Barbara Ostrom.

Ilin says the biggest design challenge was working within the home's shape, which is similar to a boomerang with two wings meeting in the kitchen. This area is used for meals and family gatherings, as well as large dinner parties.

"At 1200sq ft, the kitchen is also extremely large," says Ilin. "The design needed to contain the space – to make it cozy and functional."

For this reason, three different shaped islands, in three different finishes, were strategically placed around the kitchen. Ilin says these were designed to resemble freestanding furniture pieces that may have been collected over time.

One island, with a light-yellow paint finish and cherry wood countertop, is positioned near the refrigerator and the range, and provides a place to prepare and serve food. Another island, with a Country Burgundy paint finish, serves as a casual seating area. A third mahogany wood island offers storage and additional countertop space.

Cabinetry around the perimeter of the room features maple wood with stone countertops. In keeping with the furniture look, cabinets above the countertops are either maple or have a painted finish. Two refrigerators are integrated into a maple cabinet, designed as a traditional French armoire.

An elaborate coffered ceiling also helps to reduce the apparent scale of the kitchen, says Ilin.

Facing page: The use of five different cabinetry finishes contributes to the old-world charm of this French country kitchen. Other special features include coffered ceilings with relief inserts, a hand-made tile backsplash and a limestone-finished hood.

Above left: The kitchen, designed by Küche+Cucina, features three different shaped islands in three different finishes – Country Yellow, Country Burgundy and mahogany. The countertops are crafted from Jerusalem stone, Oro Castello granite and Spekva cherry wood.

Above: Two refrigerators are integrated into a cabinet resembling a French armoire.

Culinary color

Attention to detail and color combine to create
this bright, fresh traditional kitchen

These pages: A pale yellow color scheme complements the bright open working space of this traditional country kitchen.

Weekend retreats often provide design opportunities that homes in the city don't – such as the chance to spread out and indulge.

Architect Erica Broberg had worked with the owners of this house during a previous renovation project for their city townhouse, so she understood their desire for what they described as a calm home away from the city.

Eventually, they intend moving here permanently, so attention to details

and color co-ordination was just as important here, as it was at home.

"The owners are a very casual couple who enjoy spending a lot of time in the kitchen. They grow their own vegetables, so they requested a large traditional kitchen where they could prepare home-grown produce.

"They are also avid antique ceramic collectors, who required display space for a collection of pottery made during the 1930s and '40s."

Below: Saint Cecelia granite countertops tie in with the owners' collection of pottery.

Right: A hickory wood floor completes the traditional look of this kitchen.

Facing page: The white beadboard used in the cabinetry is repeated on the cathedral ceiling.

Broberg drew inspiration from this collection, selecting a complementary pale yellow as the main color, with Navajo white highlights.

Although the kitchen occupies an addition to a contemporary 1970s beach home, the style of the kitchen is in stark contrast – best described as turn-of-the-century Victorian villa farmhouse.

To give the home more openness and emphasize the spacious country theme, a faux cathedral-style ceiling was built inside the existing roof space.

Beadboarding, similar to that used on the cabinetry below, has been used to line the roof.

"This new raked ceiling, accentuated with recessed spot lighting, is a real treat for the owners, who have lived in the confines of flat-ceilinged city

Architect: Erica Broberg Architect, AIA
(East Hampton, NY)

Builder: Brian Mannix Construction

Windows: Pella Windows

Kitchen designer: Smith River Kitchens

Sink: Shaws Original Farm Sink

Faucets: Kraft

Oven and ventilation: Viking

Microwave: GE Profile Connection

Refrigerator: Sub-Zero

Dishwasher: Maytag

Cabinets: Crown Point Cabinets

Flooring: Hickory

Tiling: Alan Court & Associates

Photography by Kallan MacLeod, assisted by William Varsos

apartments for most of their lives," says Broberg.

To maintain the kitchen's clean-lined simplicity, the moldings around the tops of the wall-mounted cabinets are aligned with the tops of the transom windows. This creates a visual link between the two architectural details.

Along the full length of rear and side walls, a narrow built-in shelf has been extended by framing out the wall. Although this impinges on the width of the countertop, Broberg says this technique is a novel and efficient way to create additional storage space above the work area.

"This is a large kitchen, so I had a lot of space to work with. When you're working with a big blank canvas, you can design something that really sings," says Broberg.

Eclectic charm

Distinctive touches, such as antique light fittings and crafted cabinetry handles, lend an established quality to this kitchen

Left: Metal lockers are positioned vertically and horizontally above the main countertop and used as small display cabinets. These unusual pieces provide visual interest and help to create a distinctive interior.

Below: The galley design of this kitchen makes use of every space. At one end, a desk provides a barrier between the kitchen and the adjacent family living room.

Individual pieces chosen with care can transform a utilitarian space, such as a kitchen, into an aesthetically inviting interior. And often it can be objects already in the homeowners' possession which inspire an architect's vision.

That was certainly the case with this kitchen designed by architects Rehn Hassell and Marc Asmus, Yunker Associates Architecture. They took their cue from the owners' love of antiques.

"Eclectic pieces collected over time were incorporated into the design to provide the kitchen with its distinguishing characteristics," says Hassell.

In addition to found objects, such as the antique light fittings, some items were especially created in an older style. For example, the door handles on the white cabinetry are made from blackened steel. These handles feature a gun metal finish, and were crafted by a blacksmith into their distinctive shape.

Traditional touches in a mainly contemporary scheme, provide an established quality, which is particularly relevant in this kitchen. It is located in a remodeled section of an older house, originally built in the Tudor revival style.

Below: The countertops are made from Kasota stone, which is quarried in Minnesota. Adjacent to the sink countertop, narrow glass cabinets display crockery and glassware.

Facing page, top and lower left: The jewel-like quality of the antique chandelier scatters light over the breakfast banquette.

Facing page, lower right: A custom-designed panel, with a narrow bar top, shields the range and meal preparation area from the dining room. This fabricated metal panel also serves as a backsplash.

Casement windows above the main sink echo this architectural era. Their multi-pane design is complemented by two metal lockers. One is placed horizontally, the other vertically, and together they form matching display cabinets.

An ornate faucet is a point of interest on the island countertop – an area used primarily for meal preparation. A raised panel shields kitchen work from the view of guests in the dining room opposite.

This fabricated metal panel is crowned by a wood shelf that is wide enough to accommodate plates for meal service.

Interesting materials contribute additional color and texture to the interior. The countertops are made from indigenous Minnesota stone, and the wood grain on the table at the breakfast banquette matches the oak floors.

With limited floor area, banquette seating enables the table to be placed close to the wall, allowing for smooth traffic flow.

Architect: Rehn Hassell, AIA, Marc Asmus, AIA, Yunker Associates Architecture (Minneapolis, MN)

Main contractor: Lifespace

Cabinetmaker: Islero Design

Countertops: Minnesota Kasota stone from Vetter Stone

Flooring: White oak

Windows: Marvin Windows

Lighting: Decorative antique lighting and recessed halogens

Backsplash: Sink backsplash, Kasota stone; steel backsplash by Islero Design

Sink: Stainless steel, custom made

Faucets: Harrington Brass

Range: Viking

Ventilation: Aluminum turbo from Seiho

Refrigerator: Sub-Zero

Dishwasher: Asko

Photography by Kallan MacLeod

2
Hub of the home

"We live a more casual lifestyle than we did 20 years ago. Formal living and dining rooms are being replaced with spaces that allow conversation to take place with those in the kitchen, without everyone feeling they have to be in there."

Kelly Davis, architect, Sala Architects

Home entertainment

With wide, open access to other living areas, the owners of this house needn't feel left out when working in the kitchen

Preceding pages: The warm colors and lighting used throughout the house are continued in this kitchen. The owners can work in here while conversing with guests who are in the living, dining and games rooms.

Facing page: The wood countertop is a popular leaning spot for guests and doubles as a buffet.

Left and below: In addition to the large island, a bake center provides extra space for food preparation. Both work areas feature concrete countertops and pull-out benches.

Gone are the days when the cook was shut up in the kitchen preparing dinner while guests relaxed in the formal living room with an apéritif. In today's homes you are more likely to find the dinner guests chatting to the cook over the kitchen countertop.

The owners of this lakeside home wanted an open kitchen suitable for family and entertaining both small and large groups.

Designed by Kelly Davis of Sala Architects, the kitchen is at the heart of the home, opening into the living/dining and games rooms, laundry room and office. It also has direct access to an outdoor breakfast patio and enjoys uninterrupted views of the lake nearby.

A raised countertop between the kitchen and living/dining rooms provides a perfect place for guests to converse with the cook. Built from 100-year-old reclaimed red birch sourced from the bottom of Lake Superior, it features four built-in tiles framed in bronze where hot dishes can be set down. Custom-made bronze pendant lights also highlight this area.

The owners have the option of closing off the kitchen, thanks to the installation of sliding translucent glass panels in a stylized rendition of Japanese shoji screens. "When the panels are closed you get a soft glow through the glass, so it's also an indirect way of lighting the dining room," says Davis.

Because of the region's cold climate, he says it was important to use warm colors and lighting. "It makes all the difference on gray, dark days."

Red has been used as an accent color throughout the house and is continued in the stained fir kitchen island. "There is a continuity of materials throughout the house, so the kitchen integrates very well. It's not set apart with its own vocabulary of materials and detail."

Behind the island is a baking center with a backsplash featuring the same tiles that are inset into the surrounding wood countertop. Both the island and baking center have concrete countertops and pull-out benches for extra food preparation space.

Below: The kitchen enjoys wide, open access to the living areas, but can also be closed off with sliding glass panels. When closed, the translucent panels provide soft lighting for the dining area.

Facing page: Ann Sacks tiles, framed in a bronze trim, have been inset into the wood countertop. They are lit from above by custom-made bronze pendant lights.

A band of cedar containing recessed lights runs across both the kitchen and living room. The variation in ceiling height gives these spaces a different scale and character to the rest of the house.

To make the most of the view, and to ensure the contents of the kitchen are easily accessible, there are no upper cabinets. To ensure ample storage, there is a variety of drawers in the lower cabinetry.

Architect: Kelly Davis, AIA, Sala Architects (Minneapolis, MN)

Interior designer: Mary McCary, ASID, CID

Builder: Erotas Building Corporation

Cabinetry: Custom vertical grain fir from Steven Cabinets

Countertops: Concrete from Custom Rock International and red birch from Bob Kinghorn

Flooring: Concrete from Custom Rock International and red birch

Tiles: Ann Sacks

Windows: Loewen

Dining suite: Bilecky Brothers

Wallcoverings: Linen from Sonya's Place

Lighting: Iris

Sink: Blanco

Faucets: KWC

Oven and warming drawer: Thermador

Cooktop: Wolf

Ventilation: Custom

Microwave: GE

Refrigerator: Sub-Zero

Dishwasher: Fisher & Paykel

Photography by Kallan MacLeod

At the helm

Elevated above the sea, this beach house has a
galley-style kitchen with wide ocean views

Left: The island has a furniture look, in keeping with the open-plan living space. A two-tiered countertop ensures dishes are hidden from view. Lighting fixtures include pendants over the island and halogen spotlights on work areas.

Below: All the cooking appliances are on the rear wall. A dumb waiter, near the refrigerator, can be used to bring groceries up to the top floor.

Beachside living is synonymous with a casual lifestyle. Not surprisingly, this is often reflected in the architecture. Light, airy spaces that flow freely from the indoors to the outdoors are part of the beach house vernacular.

In keeping with the relaxed nature of such homes, the kitchen has a pivotal role to play, and is frequently part of a large great room.

This tropical plantation house in California is a good example. The kitchen is part of a large, open-plan family area on the top floor – the level that offers the best ocean views.

Architect Grant Kirkpatrick of KAA Architects describes the design as an inverted floor plan. This places the kitchen, the living areas and the verandahs on the top floor, with bedrooms on the second story and garaging and a beach room at ground level.

Kirkpatrick says the design needed to merge two distinct styles – the traditional Nantucket clapboard-and-shingle beach house, and the more relaxed coastal architecture of Californian West Coast.

"The family areas needed to be as open and flowing as possible, with no enclosed spaces," he says. "To this end, the white-painted wood ceiling covers the entire third story, and helps create the sense that the space is even larger than it really is. The kitchen forms part of this space, and is not hidden or tucked away from view."

These pages: The kitchen is an integral part of a large great room on the top floor. The long island is positioned to give a view of the ocean from the work area. Note that all the cooking appliances are on the rear wall.

Owner/interior designer Suzanne Ascher says the interior needed to be timeless and welcoming, as well as functional.

"We wanted the house to look as though it had been here a long time – and would look even better in another 20 years," she says. "It was also vital that the interior not detract from the spectacular view, so we have eliminated as much clutter from the kitchen as possible."

In keeping with these ideals, and to ensure the kitchen is an integral part of the overall space, the white-painted cabinetry has a furniture look.

It features traditional beadboard wood paneling, and simple Shaker-style doors and drawers with old-fashioned bin pulls. Painted moldings, cased beams and tongue-and-groove siding further enhance the simple, understated palette in the room.

To contrast the matte painted finishes, Carrara marble was specified for countertops, and white subway tiles feature on the backsplash.

"Although there is a lot of white, we wanted to avoid a monotonous look," says Kirkpatrick. "Introducing different textures, such as the glossy tiles, creates interesting shadows and reflections."

Facing page: Mismatched dining chairs add character to the great room. The family dining table is painted blue to match the sea. Interior designer and owner Suzanne Ascher says furnishings were planned with a young family in mind. Upholstered covers can be easily removed for washing.

Below: The great room opens to an outdoor room on a semi-enclosed porch. This room, which also overlooks the ocean, features a large, open fireplace. Cushion covers pick up the colors of the sand and the sea, while the exterior walls of the house are a warm, squash-gold color.

The kitchen has a long galley layout, with the main work areas and twin sinks on a long island, facing the ocean view.

"Standing at the island is like being on the helm of a ship at sea," says Kirkpatrick. "The long, buffet-style counter is also a very social space — ideal for the family to gather and entertaining guests."

Ascher says she introduced black bar stools, and black-and-white fabrics to make a strong contrast to the white walls and cabinetry.

"Every room needs a touch of black to bring it to life," she says. "Here, the very dark wood floor also provides a good contrast."

Black mismatched dining chairs continue the look, and reinforce the casual, laid-back beach lifestyle. The only other prominent color in the room is blue, which features on cushions, small appliances and the painted dining table.

"This is a very tropical shade, chosen to enhance the view of the Pacific Ocean and the sky above," says Ascher.

As well as the casual seating in the great room, Ascher has added a day bed, positioned to capture the view. And, like most Californian beach houses, there is an easy flow outdoors, to a verandah and an outdoor room, complete with open fireplace, bench seating and plumped-up cushions.

Architect: Grant Kirkpatrick, AIA, ASLA, KAA Design Group (Los Angeles, CA)

Interior designer: SEA Design

Kitchen manufacturer: Custom Cabinets

Cabinets: Painted white

Countertops: Carrara marble

Flooring: Brazilian cherry, stained Ebony

Tiling: Sonoma Tilemaker

Bar stools: SEA Design

Lighting: School House pendants

Backsplash: Subway tiles

Sink: Elkay stainless steel

Faucets: Barbara Wilson polished chrome

Oven, cooktop and ventilation: Viking

Microwave: KitchenAid

Refrigerator: Sub-Zero

Dishwasher: Miele

Photography by Kallan MacLeod

Surrounded by friends

Its clever wraparound design and central location make
this kitchen, and those using it, the center of attention

Left: Architect Mark Cashman designed this novel and compact kitchen as part of the extensions to a remodeled bungalow.

Below: The owners' travels to India provided inspiration for the kitchen's bright orange walls. These were constructed from rendered brick, then painted.

Designing a kitchen within a small space demands careful consideration. Aspects, such as layout, storage and workspace must be well planned to make the most of the area available. However, working with a limited space doesn't mean creativity need also be restricted.

Such space and budgetary constraints certainly didn't deter Mark Cashman from Marsh Cashman Koolloos Architects when he was commissioned to renovate this Californian bungalow.

Cashman recommended demolishing a series of lean-to structures at the rear of the house, to make way for a new extension that would contain the living room, kitchen and dining room, and open onto outdoor living spaces at both ends.

"With the owners' limited budget, we needed to keep the design simple," says Cashman. "They also wanted a casual, open space containing the communal living areas."

Another request from the owners

Facing page: A cabinetry unit flanks one side of the open-plan space, and contains storage and a pull-out pantry.

Left: The extensive use of stainless steel gives the kitchen a clean, commercial look.

Below: In addition to a skylight above the kitchen, task lighting is provided by brick lights set into the backsplash.

was for something a little unusual. So, rather than opting for the ubiquitous island countertop, the architect designed a central block with the kitchen area defined by two, half–height, orange-painted walls.

This compact design allows those using the kitchen to socialize with guests while preparing meals, yet it keeps any mess well hidden from the lounge and dining room.

This central block houses the sink, cooker and dishwasher, in two parallel workspaces that feature built–in stainless steel countertops and backsplashes. A custom stainless steel hood is built into the roof structure above.

"The use of stainless steel gives the kitchen a commercial feel, and reflects the owner's involvement in the catering industry," says Cashman.

Off to one side of the kitchen block, a large bank of cabinetry runs the length of the space. It contains the pantry, an integrated fridge and microwave, and storage for crockery.

Architect and kitchen designer: Mark Cashman and Steve Koolloos, Marsh Cashman Koolloos Architects
Cabinets: Polyurethane and Black Japan stain
Countertops, backsplash and sink: Custom stainless steel
Flooring: Chocolate-brown-colored concrete
Paints: Dulux
Lighting: Mondoluce
Oven and cooktop: Smeg
Refrigerator: Fisher & Paykel
Dishwasher: Miele
Ventilation: Qasair
Hot water system: Rinnai

Photography by Mark Mawson

Curvaceous

This circular kitchen, at heart of the family quarters,
is designed to be a flexible environment

Every home has public and private spaces – areas in which you can formally entertain guests and rooms where you can put your feet up and relax. Those informal parts of the home often incorporate the kitchen – it's the room where the family can congregate while the meals are prepared.

The kitchen featured here is in a penthouse apartment that enjoys spectacular views of San Francisco Bay. The plans called for a circular layout and interior designer Nestor Matthews embraced the concept because the kitchen functions as the hub of the informal living areas.

"It's open to the family room, open to the breakfast area and because it is round, everything is within easy reach," he says.

In the center of the kitchen is a circular island that is specifically intended for meal preparation. Above the granite countertop is a ventilation system that integrates with the ceiling cove above.

"By placing fluorescent lighting inside the ceiling cove, the working area is sufficiently illuminated, without being too bright," Matthews says.

There are clearly defined zones within the kitchen for various activities. Beside the entrance to the family room is a

Below: The circular layout ensures everything is within easy reach. The central island is intended for meal preparation, while the outer axis has the refrigerator, oven and washing up area.

Right: The kitchen is the hub of the family area in this penthouse apartment. Its open-ended design enables those working in it to view the plasma screen in the neighboring room.

Facing page: A custom-designed banquette is intended as a breakfast area.

Photography by Kallan MacLeod

small sink intended for drinks preparation. On the opposite side of the room is a separate countertop for washing up.

The kitchen itself is distinguished by bird's-eye maple cabinetry, dyed a translucent green, that complements the cherry wood paneling in the family room. In addition, the herringbone floor is bordered by dark oak wood that delineates the area between the kitchen and family room.

On the other side of the kitchen a custom-designed breakfast banquette is curved against the glass wall to echo the circular theme. The banquette encloses the room without interfering visually with the magnificent view.

Interior designers: Nestor Matthews, DJ Pak, Dane Robert Wilson, Allison Grant, Matthews Studio (San Francisco, CA)

Space planning: Nestor Bradley

Cabinetry/construction: Ryan Associates

Countertops and backsplash: Fox Marble

Faucets: Grohe

Refrigerator and wine cooler: Sub-Zero

Hood: Best

Oven: Dacor

Cooktop: Thermador

Banquette table top: Julian Giuntoli

Banquette: Lucarini; Lee Jofa; Christopher Hyland

3
Contemporary design

"The endless design qualities and durability of concrete make it my preferred material for the modern kitchen."

Fu Tung Cheng, designer, Cheng Design

Solid foundation

An old brick fireplace – once used as a barbecue – was the starting point for the design of this kitchen

Preceding pages: Before remodeling, this kitchen had small windows above the sink counter, and cupboards separating it from the dining area. With new windows and less separation, the kitchen is now light and airy.

Left: A stainless steel countertop on one side of this kitchen offsets the rich, natural tones of the concrete countertop on the opposite wall.

Below: The designer has retained the original fireplace as a feature of the kitchen and modernized it by encasing the old brick hearth in concrete.

Every design ultimately draws its inspiration from somewhere or something, whether it is obvious or more subtle.

The original 1950s kitchen in this home featured an open brick fireplace on a brick hearth above the countertop – once used as a brazier or barbecue.

Although the fire hadn't been used in many years, designer Fu Tung Cheng seized on it as an inspiration for the design of the new kitchen.

"I decided to retain the brick hearth below the fire as a focal point, and used it to create a sense of mass in the

kitchen," says the designer.

The countertop was then extended across the full length of the back wall of the kitchen. As well as the open fire, the counter includes the cooktop, with a ventilation hood over its center.

The thickness of the old hearth dictated the finished depth of the new countertop. The bricks were covered in a polished concrete casing, creating an imposing, 12in-thick countertop.

Finishing the countertop in concrete,

allowed Cheng to incorporate some individualized details. For example, Russian dolomite crystals and a fossilized ammonite are embedded in the surface.

On a more practical level, brass bars, in the shape of a Chinese geomancy symbol, based on a hexagram and representing 'grace', form a trivet for hot pots and pans.

As a contrasting element to the concrete, the counter on the other

side of the kitchen is made from stainless steel. A marble slab, inset into the peninsula, is framed in polished concrete.

A concrete end wall on the peninsula anchors the countertop to the floor and visually links it to the other side of the kitchen.

Flat-paneled cabinetry, made from vertical-grained plyboo, and a light-colored plywood, complements the sheen of the stainless steel and the

Kitchen designer: Fu Tung Cheng, Cheng Design (Berkeley, CA)

Cabinetmaker: Peter Malakoff

Cabinetry: Plyboo doors, maple boxes

Countertops: Geocrete, designed by Cheng Design; stainless steel from Berlin Food Equipment Co

Flooring: Plyboo from Smith & Fong

Backsplash: Architectonics ceramic tiles from Waterworks; Loom ceramic tiles from Ann Sacks

Windows: Cheng Design in mahogany

Lighting: Tech Lighting

Sink: Stainless steel

Faucets: Grohe Ladylux Café in Chrome Black

Refrigerator, oven, warming drawer and microwave: GE Monogram

Cooktops: Gaggenau

Ventilation: Vent-A-Hood

Dishwasher: Miele

Photography by Tim Maloney

stronger tones of the concrete.

"We have used natural materials throughout the kitchen, because they add calmness and warmth to the space," says Cheng. "Combining these materials with natural colors, like the green of the mosaic tiles, terra cotta and maize, gives the kitchen an earthy, organic quality," he says.

While the new kitchen has much the same footprint as its predecessor, Cheng opened up the windows to allow more light in the dining area and redefined the wall between the kitchen and rest of the house.

"We cut back the separating wall to create a visual connection between the two areas.

"The original kitchen was dark and closed off, and it felt cramped and oppressive. Now, because it has an open, light and airy feeling, the kitchen harmonizes with the rest of the house," Cheng says.

Above left: The open feeling of the kitchen is enhanced by the large windows in the dining space. With the wall between the spaces gone, the cook can enjoy the views and light that pours in through the dining windows. The owners and designer favored mainly natural colors, such as green, terra cotta and maize, and raw materials like concrete, wood and marble.

Middle: The colorful oblong mark in the countertop occurred naturally when the concrete top was poured.

Above right: Brass bars, in a hexagram, based on Chinese geomancy, are set into the concrete countertop and form a trivet for hot pots.

Pure and simple

Pared-back design and hidden storage solutions make this
kitchen an unassuming backdrop to a lively living area

Facing page and left: The kitchen is on one side of a large living area that was formerly three small rooms. Monckton says it was designed for practicality and features low-maintenance materials.

Below: The white Corian countertop features an integrated sink for a smooth, seamless finish. For this reason also, the countertop has a fine, mitered edge, rather than the traditional lip.

To make a strong design statement a kitchen doesn't have to be large, or feature lots of detailing and a variety of finishes. Sometimes, less really is more, as the kitchen on these pages illustrates.

Designed by architect Peter Monckton for his own home, the kitchen is a lesson in orderliness, with a design that is pared back to essentials.

The new kitchen is part of the major renovation of a 1920s duplex, which created one large living area from three small rooms. As the house is close to the ocean, Monckton says he wanted to create a relaxed, casual feel and borrow the traditional beach house concept of placing a kitchen along one wall.

"We wanted the kitchen to play a secondary role to the living areas, hence its simple, pared-back design," he says. "The kitchen needed to be a neutral backdrop, with artworks and colorful furnishings providing the focus of attention."

A single 18ft-long Corian countertop and a bank of cabinetry are positioned against one wall. With metallic-painted cabinets above the countertop concealing all the small appliances, the only detailing in the kitchen is the small knob handles of the doors and a single faucet. Monckton says even the Corian countertop, which has an integrated sink, features a fine, mitered edge, rather than a lip.

The cabinet doors immediately above the countertop lift to expose appliances and power outlets, while the next row of cabinets provides storage for crockery and glasses. White-painted drawers below the countertop are used for pot storage.

A floor-to-ceiling black, color-backed glass panel and backsplash at the left end of the kitchen help ensure the larger appliances are discreetly positioned.

Monckton says the cabinets, the countertop, and a narrow skylight create

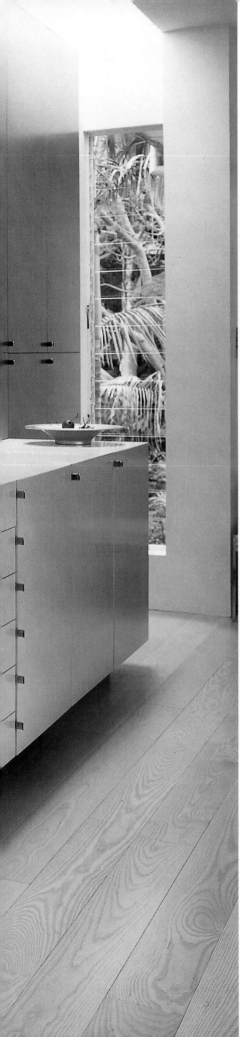

Left: Architect Peter Monckton designed a series of planes that intersect the volume of the space, enhancing a crisp, contemporary look.

Below: This kitchen in a refurbished duplex has been reduced to its bare essentials – a wall of white- and metallic-painted cabinetry, which conceals appliances.

a series of planes within the volume of the space. Sections that appear to have been sliced away add to the overall composition.

This effect is further enhanced by a mirrored kickboard that is recessed four inches, which makes the lower cabinetry appear to float within the greater living space.

Architect: Peter Monckton, RAIA, Monckton Fyfe

Cabinets: Metallic and white polyurethane

Countertops and integrated sink: Corian

Flooring: European ash floating floor

Backsplash: Color-backed glass

Faucet: Borma

Oven and cooktop: Smeg

Ventilation: Qasair

Photography by Simon Kenny

Visual trickery

A few subtle, clever modifications have created a feeling
of space and openness in this small apartment

Facing page: Where space is at a premium, it must be used carefully. This dining table in this kitchen slides away into the island when it's not in use.

Below: Tall cupboards provide storage for the dining chairs when they aren't needed.

In cities today, land is at a premium. As a consequence, apartments tend to be small. Using one or two innovative design tricks allows a good designer to get the best possible value out of the available space.

Designer Leong Yinghow was asked to renovate the kitchen of a very compact apartment. The tiny, U-shaped kitchen was enclosed and separated from the main living area, which was also small.

"To make the most of both the kitchen and living room, visual trickery was called for," says Yinghow.

The designer removed the walls separating the kitchen from the living area, making both spaces appear larger.

"We then used a screen divider to block part of the kitchen so it was not in direct view of the front entrance. To ensure the screen does not dominate the space, it has a window in it," he says.

At 8ft high, the ceilings in the apartment are quite low. To make them look higher, the screen is made from vertical slats of wood.

Because the kitchen is now part of the living area, the space is freed up to be used for a variety of activities.

A retractable dining table has been specially designed to give the room extra flexibility. When folded into the island countertop it occupies only 3ft of space. However, a ball-bearing mechanism allows it to be pulled out to become a 6ft-long table, which seats up to eight guests.

Floor-to-ceiling cabinets run the full length of one wall in the kitchen and living area providing storage for a variety of items including up to eight dining chairs.

"In this way, the space becomes very flexible. The owners can have the table

Below: The owners enjoy entertaining friends, both formally and informally. When the dining table is fully open, it is long enough to seat eight people. For smaller, more casual gatherings, the table can be retracted and the kitchen island used as a buffet.

Right: With the table extended, the kitchen flows seamlessly into the living area.

Facing page: The vertically ribbed wall blocks the view of the kitchen from the entrance to the apartment. However, a small window in the partition ensures the kitchen does not feel closed in.

Kitchen designer: Leong Yinghow

Cabinets: Quarter-cut oak with polyurethane finish; clear lacquer

Flooring: Existing cream marble

Faucets: Grohe

Oven: Siemens

Cooktop: DeDietrich Domino induction cooktop

Refrigerator: Fisher & Paykel

Sofa: Montis

Photography by Tim Nolan

fully opened up and ready for a dinner party for eight. Or the table and chairs can be completely away, freeing up the space for a more casual party. Then, the island counter in the kitchen acts as a buffet where food and drinks can be served," says the designer.

Other elements of the design also make the space look larger. A roller door conceals small appliances so the kitchen never looks cluttered, and long,

narrow cabinets set higher than usual above the sink make the kitchen look wider. Drawers in the kitchen are extra-wide for the same reason, side cabinets are cantilevered off the wall and island counter is on legs to create a lighter look.

"Cabinetry is in a light-colored veneer with the grain carefully laid on the horizontal to widen the space," says Yinghow.

Social hub

An open, functional kitchen with clean lines
completes this modern family home

Left: All plumbing and electrical connections are concealed in the 3in-wide legs of the island.

Below: Morgan Cronin from Cronin Kitchens designed this kitchen with family living in mind. The floating island doubles as a place for the children to do their homework and eat meals.

Open-plan living tends to bring the family together – even when they're engaging in different activities. This trend often influences contemporary design.

The owners of this home wanted a kitchen where members of their family could gather for meals. They also wanted to be able to supervise the children's homework while preparing the evening meal.

Designer Morgan Cronin's brief was to create a kitchen featuring stainless steel countertops and dark wood cabinetry. He was also asked to include the owners' existing refrigerator and microwave.

The focal point of the kitchen is the uplit floating island. Cronin says having the island floating off the floor visually reduces its bulkiness and softens the impact it has on the surrounding space.

Because Cronin was brought in at an early stage of construction, he was able to have the plumbing and electrical connections positioned so they could be concealed in the 3in-wide legs of the island.

Below: Chunky stainless steel end panels match the countertops, while dark wooden cabinetry complements the owners' black refrigerator.

Facing page: The frosted glass crockery cabinets provide plenty of storage space.

Within a 2in space are waste and water pipes, halogen lights, and gas and electrical connections.

Installation of the island proved to be challenge, says Cronin. "The island was in one piece because I didn't want any joins in it. It took six men to lift it off the truck. We laid it upside down, next to its final position, so we could install the steel reinforcing beams and cabinetry. We then rolled the island over into its final resting place."

Chocolate-stained Victorian white ash cabinetry was used, complementing the owners' black refrigerator. To lighten the heavy effect, frosted glass was used to accentuate the lift-up cabinetry doors above the hob area.

"The floor is also Victorian white ash, ensuring there is consistency in texture,

but also lightening the effect of the dark wood," says Cronin.

The kitchen was originally designed as a galley-style kitchen. But to meet the owners' need for extra storage space, the island and hob area were reduced in size to make way for crockery cabinets.

By using frosted glass on the cabinets, balance between the refrigerator and pantry areas, and symmetry between the hob and island areas were retained. The cabinets also form a wall, hiding the sliding door from the kitchen to the entranceway.

The height of the cabinetry on either side of the hob was designed to exactly accommodate the lift-up doors above the hob area. The bulkhead above it provides a ceiling for the sliding door track to slot into.

Architect (house): Shanahan Architects

Kitchen designer/manufacturer: Morgan Cronin, Cronin Kitchens

Interior designer: Prudence Lane

Cabinets: Chocolate-stained Victorian white ash

Hardware: Hettich Innotech

Countertops: Stainless steel

Flooring: Victorian white ash

Backsplash: Stained ash and stainless steel

Stove, extractor: AEG

Hob: Ilve

Dishwasher: Fisher & Paykel DishDrawers

Refrigerator: Kenmore

Microwave: Panasonic

Waste unit: In-Sink-Erator

Photography by Kallan MacLeod

Pared back

Reducing this kitchen to the bare essentials helped determine its ergonomic layout

In many coastal areas, the traditional idea of a beach house has given way to something far more contemporary. This house is a prime example, and nowhere is this more evident than in the kitchen, which is part of a top-floor great room.

Designed for an environmentalist, the house is built from environmentally correct materials – mainly steel, glass and stone. This philosophy is reinforced by a Bulthaup System 20 kitchen, which has aluminum cabinets, a stainless steel island and countertops, and two mobile stainless steel units.

Kitchen designer Chris Tosdevin says the owner appreciated the Bulthaup design approach, whereby all the elements of the kitchen are determined by their functionality.

"The house itself is a modernist architectural classic, and it was important that the kitchen continue this theme," he says. "The owner wanted to reduce it to its bare essentials, with no excess clutter. The basic functions of chopping, washing and cooking are accommodated within a highly ergonomic design."

Kitchen designer: Chris Tosdevin, AIA, Bulthaup (Los Angeles, CA)

Kitchen manufacturer: Bulthaup

Cabinets: Aluminum and stainless steel

Countertops and backsplash: Stainless steel

Wallcoverings: Translucent glass

Sink: Integrated in countertop

Faucets: Bulthaup

Oven and steam oven: Miele

Cooktop: Gaggenau

Refrigerator: Sub-Zero

Dishwasher: Miele

Mobile trash cart: Bulthaup

Photography by John Ellis

A long, stainless steel island that appears to float within the space, is the main work countertop. This features a cooktop and two sinks, including a shallow sink with guides to accommodate a mandoline slicing and shredding device. Steel cross bars on the island are a visual link with the steel framing of the house, which can be seen through the large, opaque glass side walls.

This light, streamlined look is further reinforced by the aluminum cabinets. These incorporate a Miele oven and steam oven, a fully integrated dishwasher and refrigerator, a tall pull-out pantry and an appliance garage.

"To eliminate clutter, the storage is very specific, and place settings are limited," says Tosdevin.

Two mobile units, including a trash cabinet, can be tucked beneath the island when not in use.

Above left and above: Stainless steel and aluminum are the key materials in this Bulthaup 20 kitchen on the top floor of a contemporary beach house. Designed on environmental principles, the kitchen places an emphasis on streamlined functionality.

What's hot?

Horizontal lines, flush surfaces and high-gloss finishes
are the key kitchen trends from Europe this season

Despite the wealth of design talent in America, it's always interesting to see the new design directions coming out of Europe. After all, these trends influence the materials, colors and products that go into our own kitchens.

Ross Longney, a distributor of European Alno and Poggenpohl kitchens, says there is a strong move back to high-gloss finishes, and towards man-made materials.

"Shiny surfaces even extend to the use of glass for countertops, as well as backsplashes and cabinetry doors," he says. "Other man-made materials, such as laminates and quartz-based countertops, are also popular. Quartz products allow for very thin countertops, which enhance the horizontal lines of a kitchen – and that's also a particularly strong design trend."

Longney says there is a greater dominance of aluminum, noticeable in trim, handles and appliances. But while man-made materials are in favor, there are some strong wood elements, notably highly patterned veneers that appear as accents in a kitchen. These are often repeated in adjacent living areas.

"Extending the kitchen units into the living areas is another trend," he says. "Kitchens no longer exist solely on their own. In many homes and apartments, similar cabinetry is designed to accommodate home theater systems and shelving."

The reversal is also true – technology is now being accommodated in the kitchen. LCD televisions are often wall mounted, and stands are provided for computers.

In other trends, cabinetry is recessed into the wall to provide a flush finish. Brighter colors are being seen, notably red and black with silver. And there's a new product called Picture Line that enables a screen of any image to be imprinted onto cabinetry – perhaps the ultimate customization.

Left: This new Alno kitchen from Europe is typical of current design trends. The high-gloss finish of the cabinetry, the color and the aluminum trim are features increasingly seen in European kitchens. Glass doors and screens, and recessed cabinetry are other key elements.

Open house

A simple, minimalist color scheme ensures this kitchen, living and dining space form one large and cohesive open area

Left: An open-plan space contains the kitchen, living area and dining table in this contemporary apartment by architect Jon Johannsen. A large marble island is strategically positioned to ensure the cook can enjoy the view while preparing a meal.

Below: Large slabs of marble highlight the countertop. This helps to make the island look like a piece of furniture.

While a kitchen is clearly an essential part of any home, it needn't always take center stage. This is especially true when other elements, such as views, also deserve attention.

The kitchen and living space of this new apartment, overlooking a popular city beach, lent itself to a very simple and minimal design treatment. Architect Jon Johannsen was asked to create a contemporary, open-plan interior that ensured the views could be enjoyed from all living spaces.

The kitchen is sited at the rear of the large living space, but is designed so it looks towards the view across the dining table and living area. Louver blinds can be angled in to catch the view and cut out neighboring houses.

White and natural materials, such as wood and marble, plus stainless steel dominate the living spaces, creating the streamlined interior the owners wanted.

"To help the kitchen blend into the living area, the cabinets are designed to resemble pieces of furniture, and are finished in similar colors and materials to the rest of the space," says Johannsen.

To add interest to the far end of the living space and counterbalance the view, slabs of white marble, veined with black, were used to wrap round three sides of the island, including the countertop.

"As well as adding a bold aesthetic to the room, the marble suggests images of foamy waves breaking on the sand," says the architect.

The large square island is also multi-functional. It can be used as a buffet for entertaining, a breakfast bar, or as a meeting point where the owners can prepare a meal while guests sit on the other side and enjoy a drink.

To ensure the marble island is the focus of the kitchen, the work surface along the perimeter wall is a simple stainless steel countertop. The undercounter cabinetry and refrigerator are also finished in stainless steel. For the same reasons, the high level cabinets are finished in a translucent resin, while the backsplash is made from white, back-painted glass.

Architect: Architects Johannsen + Associates

Interior designer: John Montemurro

Windows: Aluminum with Dulux Charcoal Duratec powdercoat

Cabinets: Lower doors: stainless steel; upper doors: translucent resin; worktop and pantry: polyurethane paint with Dulux gloss Antique White

Countertops: Stainless steel; Calacatta marble slab with honed finish

Flooring: Spotted gum; limestone slab

Lighting: Targetti recessed halogen lamps with cool beam downlights

Backsplash: Glass

Sink: Stainless steel

Oven, cooktop, ventilation, dishwasher: Gaggenau

Refrigerator: Amana Stainless Steel

Photography by Simon Kenny

Facing page: With a translucent resin finish, the upper cupboards in the kitchen are unobtrusive in the living space.

Above left: For simplicity, the appliances and the undercounter cabinetry are stainless steel.

Top: Large drawers in the island provide good storage space for crockery, pots and pans.

Above: A splash of color is added with the flowers in a small alcove in the back wall of the kitchen.

4

For the serious cook

"Every step of the design process is a pleasure when you are working with a homeowner who encourages and demands quality."

Michael Graham, architect, Liederbach & Graham Architects

Preceding pages: Divided into zones, in keeping with Jewish dietary laws, this kitchen contains seven ovens, two warming drawers and three dishwashers.

Below: In the intermediate preparation area the sink is carved into the countertop, along with a groove for the marble chopping board.

Right: Rough-hewn stone on the wall matches stone taken from the foundations of this 1908 house.

That food is more than just fuel for our bodies is testimony to how far civilization has evolved. Ways of preparing, cooking and eating meals are a practical expression of our culture. So, when ancient religious practice combines with a passion for fine cuisine, the ingredients are set for a dynamic kitchen design.

In keeping with Jewish dietary laws, architect Michael Graham divided the main area of this kitchen into four distinct zones – meat, intermediate, dairy and cooking.

"In kosher cooking, all the utensils, pots, pans and plates must be separated at the preparation stage and at the washing up stages, but it all comes together in the middle – during the cooking."

Each of these preparation zones has a distinguishing feature. The countertop intended for meat preparation has a foot pedal that operates the faucet in a similar manner to a surgeon's sink. The intermediate area has a 5in-deep granite sink, carved into the countertop – a shrewd detail, which, Graham says, is technically difficult to achieve.

Epicurean's delight

Gourmet cuisine is prepared in this multi-zoned kitchen in accordance
with kosher law

Facing page: The butler's pantry is situated in the secondary part of the L-shaped kitchen. It has a pizza oven and bread oven. Nickel-plated light fittings, with incandescent lamps and prismatic glass, cast a soft glow over the island countertop. Plates are stowed inside the island.

Left: This kitchen design is a fine balance between traditional materials and modern details. Poised above every preparation area, there is a thin glass shelf, on which are placed items such cooking oils and condiments. A telephone and small desk are located beside the range.

Below: A stainless steel roller door conceals an appliance garage. The spice rack is close at hand for when the chef is assembling meals at the island.

The dairy countertop has a steam oven, and the cooking area has a range that contains two ovens, a grill and a French simmer plate. There are a total of seven ovens and two warming drawers in the kitchen.

Visually, Graham contrasts the sleek aesthetic of technically advanced kitchen equipment with natural materials and handcrafted objects.

"It is a balanced composition of traditional elements, such as the reclaimed limestone floors and ceramics, with very modern elements, such as glass shelving and stainless steel appliances."

Attention to small details is another distinguishing characteristic of the kitchen interior. For example, the cherry cabinetry is echoed in profiled wooden moldings above the antique light fixtures in both the main kitchen and the butler's pantry.

This latter area forms the secondary part of the L-shaped kitchen – its large island used for assembling each course before it is taken into the dining room. Although, as the homeowner points out, when you have a multifunctional kitchen the conviviality begins well before the meal is served.

"We've had parties with over twelve people, where everyone was in the kitchen preparing food that we are all able to share."

Architect: Michael Graham, Stasia Hazard, Liederbach & Graham Architects (Chicago, IL)

Interior designer: Anthony Catalfano Interiors

Window manufacturer: Krumpen Woodworks

Kitchen manufacturer: Bulthaup

Floor and counter stone: Fordham Marble

Floor: Paris Ceramics

Cabinets: Cherry wood from Bulthaup

Island top, countertops and backsplash: Dakota mahogany granite

Faucets: Waterworks

Intermediate sink: Custom granite, with sink accessories from Bulthaup

Foot pedal: Pedalworks

Butler's pantry sink: Blanco

Refrigerators: Traulsen and Sub-Zero

Freezer: Traulsen

Range: Le Grand Palais from La Cornue

Remote blowers: Greenheck

Wall oven and steam oven: Gaggenau

Warming drawers: Dacor

Dishwashers: Miele, with front panels from Bulthaup

Disposer: KitchenAid

Dairy faucet: Waterworks

Photography by Kallan MacLeod, assisted by William Varsos

Chef's corner

When fine food and entertaining are an important part of your lifestyle, a kitchen that caters to every occasion is essential

Left: The simple layout of this kitchen ensures maximum storage and counter space. Dark colored cabinetry provides a striking contrast to the cream-colored marble floors and walls.

Below: Stainless steel appliances provide a visual accent to the gray, black and white color scheme. The countertop is a 1in-thick sheet of stainless steel with negative detailing underneath.

Can true chefs ever retire? Sure, they may hang up their hat when they stop collecting their pay check, but if they've been preparing meals to the highest standard, how can they stop when it's no longer a job? The truth is, cooking is more than a profession, it's a passion, and most chefs don't lower their standards just because they are cooking at home.

When John Borwick and Gary Withers bought their new home, the kitchen design was of utmost importance to Borwick, a former chef. He had already purchased the appliances, and he wanted a kitchen fit for a professional, yet welcoming for guests.

Kitchen designer Ingrid Geldof designed a layout to enable Borwick to be part of the conversation, without his guests interfering in his space.

Facing page and left : Behind the opaque glass doors, a butler's pantry houses a counter, sink, refrigerator and other appliances, such as a coffee maker. There is also storage for food, alcohol and glassware. A speaker placed above the refrigerator enables the chef to listen to music as he works.

Below: The kitchen is nestled into one corner of the L-shaped living area. Dividing the kitchen and living rooms is an island. It provides seating for guests, who can chat with the chef without disturbing meal preparation.

"The island divides the kitchen from the living room so that guests can be seated at the stools, chat to the chef, yet not be in the way. Alternatively they can be seated at the dining table," Geldof says.

In the kitchen, there is a very clear demarcation of preparation space. Appliances, such as the oven and dishwasher, sit beneath the countertop flanking the outer wall. Opposite, the island countertop is mainly used to serve the meals, as the crockery is stored in cupboards beneath.

On the far wall, next to the fridge, opaque glass doors conceal a butler's pantry. This area houses another preparation counter, a sink and a fridge, plus storage for glassware, alcohol and food items.

"The advantage of the butler's pantry is that it can be used for food preparation during a party and the mess is concealed simply by closing the door," says Geldof.

Kitchen utensils, displayed on either side of the stove, are easy to reach during cooking and provide visual appeal against the dark-colored wall and iron glass backsplash. The drawers beside the oven are specifically designed to house cooking oils and other condiments.

"Logical placement of utensils and clever storage ideas increase the efficiency of a kitchen," says Geldof.

Kitchen designer: Ingrid Geldof and Amanda Smith, Ingrid Geldof Design

Cabinetry: Lacquered with paint finish

Countertops: Satin stainless steel; black polished granite

Backsplash: Low iron glass

Oven and stove: Rosieres

Ventilation: Qasair

Icemaker: Gaggenau

Refrigerator: Fisher & Paykel

Dishwasher: Asko stainless steel

Photography by Suellen Boag

Command post

With its sheer volume of space and abundance of natural
light, this kitchen makes a powerful impact

Facing page: This ranch-style kitchen is characterized by its large beams, windows and high ceilings.

Left: Natural light from the large window above the sink fills the kitchen, making it seem even more spacious and open. This window also provides a view to the front garden.

Below: The Viking cooker and the white-tiled rangehood enclosure dominate the kitchen.

Whether it's large or small, a space needs to be well-proportioned to look good. So, when you plan a large kitchen, you need to consider not only the amount of counter and cabinet space, but also the height of the ceiling and the size of the windows.

Architect Russell Shubin was asked to design a new kitchen and casual breakfast area for the owners of a ranch-style home.

"The owner is a keen cook who also enjoys baking, so within the kitchen we needed to make provision for these functions," Shubin says.

"Essentially, we added a section onto the house which contains the new kitchen, a casual living space with an outdoor patio. The architecture of these new spaces had to integrate with the rest of the house."

"We wanted to create a light-filled, airy space for the kitchen," says Shubin. "To achieve this, we used exposed ceiling trusses and installed a large skylight into the ceiling above the island."

The kitchen is organized along a central axis that begins with the large granite-topped island. The termination point at the far end of the kitchen is an imposing rangehood enclosure that provides ventilation for the Viking range.

"The rangehood enclosure is a dominant feature in the kitchen. The face is finished in white tiles to enhance its height.

"To maintain the proportions of the space, we added a large window to the side wall above the sink. This window, together with the rangehood enclosure, large island, windows, trusses and the skylight, are in proportion to the scale of the room. These details are also very much in keeping with the ranch style of the existing house," Shubin says.

To complement the owners' collection of Arts and Crafts-style furniture in the living and dining areas, the kitchen cabinetry has been finished in rich

Left: The island includes a countertop at two levels – one for cooking preparation and a lower one with seating.

Below: A small nook to the left of the kitchen provides space for a breakfast table and chairs. Doors open onto a courtyard.

cherry wood, with geometric detailing and iron hardware.

Another distinctively Arts and Crafts touch comes from the arched overhang above the rangehood enclosure and the handcrafted tiles behind the stove. The design for this corner draws its inspiration from an open hearth, Shubin says.

To maintain the lines and form of the kitchen, downlighting is integrated into the beams.

Architect: Shubin + Donaldson Architects, AIA (Los Angeles and Santa Barbara, CA)

Main contractor: Paster Construction

Interior designer: Andrew Zeff, Dzign

Flooring: All American Floors

Window coverings: Fabric from J Stephens & Co

Fabrication: Icona Draperies; Martha's Upholstery

Dining tables and chairs: Stickley Furniture Co

Backsplash: Pratt and Larson tiles from Country Floors

Range, microwave, refrigerator, dishwasher and waste unit: Viking

Photography by Kallan MacLeod

Seriously appealing

If you want a kitchen fit for professionals,
design the room around the chef

These pages: In this kitchen, designed for serious cooking, the appliances are commercial grade. But while large ovens, double hobs and a custom-made extractor fan enable catering for large groups, concession has been made to aesthetic appeal. For example, the countertops are granite rather than the stainless steel normally found in professional kitchens.

Although today's kitchen is a highly functional room, it also a popular space in which to congregate. An accomplished chef requires the tools of the professional without sacrificing the aesthetic appeal of a contemporary home.

Owners Mike and Ann Spratt asked interior designer Leon Bieldt to create a 'serious' kitchen – a room that contained commercial grade appliances without compromising on style.

"We had to marry professional functionality with a look that was smart and enhanced the view across the ocean," Mike Spratt says.

Bieldt began by installing a large L-shaped island in the center of the room. This provided two practical countertops. On the corner sits a double sink. Below it is an industrial dishwasher that cleans in seconds.

The wall opposite the island is dominated by a large oven and stovetop, with custom-made extractor fan. The clear glass backsplash enables the chef to look out into the courtyard on the other side. Although the cook has their back to the ocean, they can still see out of the room, Spratt says.

Suspended from the ceiling is a large, white canopy with a track of halogen lights above the hob and sink. The ceiling has been painted black to enhance the canopy's sculptural impact.

With a separate pantry room, ample storage space for utensils and dishes is provided by drawers and cupboards. Rather than chunky handles that might catch on clothing, rectangle aluminum pulls are set into the light gray cabinets.

Spratt says they installed large drawers below the countertops so that their contents would be more accessible than

cupboards that require you to bend down to see into.

To add visual contrast to the light gray cabinetry and aluminum, the floor is a Jarrah wood that has been stained black. The same Jarrah is used for the back of the island. Spratt says that it is here that guests can rest a glass of wine and talk to those preparing the meal – without interrupting their work.

These pages: Ample storage space is provided by drawers in the island and cupboards above the microwave. At the far end of the room a trolley contains drainage trays that can be attached to the sink during dishwashing, then wheeled out of sight when not required. The kitchen is large, with floor-to-ceiling windows so that both the chef and the guests can enjoy the ocean view while the meal is being prepared.

Interior designer: Leon Bieldt, Draw The Line Studio

Architectural concept: Simon Carnachan

Cabinets: Two-pot spray lacquer

Drawer pulls: Häfele

Flooring: Stained Jarrah

Backsplash: Glass

Faucets: Ideal Standard

Oven and cooktop: Falcon

Refrigerator: Sub-Zero

Dishwasher: Starline

Waste unit: Whirlaway Kenmore trash compactor

Microwave: Sharp

Espresso machine: Jura

Photography by Kallan MacLeod

Sweeping statement

When you're passionate about cooking, functionality is everything. Modern chefs' kitchens are strong on detail, with customized storage and secondary food prep areas

These pages: The long, curved island in this chef's kitchen provides a casual seating area for family members or guests at cooking demonstrations.

Space can be a luxury when you're planning a new kitchen in an existing house. But for passionate cooks, it's a priority – even if it means knocking down walls to achieve it.

For the owners of the new kitchen featured on these pages, a large space was necessary to accommodate all the features required. Fortunately, the proportions of the Victorian house suited their need for a combined kitchen and dining area, and a separate scullery.

Keith Sheedy of Focal Kitchens says the kitchen was designed to meet the immediate needs of a young family, but it was also planned for the future, so the owner Robyn Harris could host cooking classes for small groups.

"A long, curved island was designed to provide the necessary counter space, and to ensure family or guests didn't have to sit in a straight line," says Sheedy. "The curve is a more friendly shape, allowing people to interact with each other as well as the chef."

The sheer size of the 16ft-long island created some design challenges, however.

"Even though we had the benefit of a large space and high ceiling, the island could have looked massive," says Sheedy. "To avoid this, each edge of countertop was curved on a different radius. This means it is 12in wider at one end, where it extends over the cabinetry, creating room for the seating area."

The size of the countertop also determined the use of Corian, the only suitable surface material that could be formed without a break.

Below: To help reduce the size of the island, the countertop is curved to extend out from one end of the island only, providing room for stools.

Right: Cherry veneer drawers and sage-gray lacquered cabinets provide a neutral contrast to the white walls of the kitchen.

"To make the whole island appear less imposing, we also added legs to the seating end, so the floor flows under it creating a more open feel," says Sheedy.

The island features a glass-fronted dishwasher and cherry veneer drawers with customized crockery storage. A two-pack polyurethane finish in sage gray highlights the rest of the cabinetry.

"We chose neutral tones to let the materials speak for themselves," says Sheedy. "The subtle contrast is a sophisticated look, which suited our purposes."

A separate, enclosed cooking center opposite the island features Gaggenau countertop modules. These include a steamer, grill, wok burner and two ceramic burners. There is also a faucet to fill the steamer, which is plumbed for drainage.

Overhead cherry cabinetry, either side of the hood, has sandblasted glass doors. Drawers beneath the stainless steel countertop are specifically designed for pots and pans of different heights. There is also a working cabinet, which accommodates cooking oils and spices. Sheedy says items are positioned at their point of use, to provide maximum functionality.

Another bank of cabinetry opposite the island incorporates a large fridge-freezer and two ovens – one a steam oven.

An opening between the two walls of cabinetry leads to a scullery – a long room that runs the width of the kitchen behind these cabinets.

Sheedy says this room was designed to provide a second food preparation area, so more than one chef could work in the kitchen at the same time. This room features additional counter space and a second sink. There is also a refrigerated wine cellar, microwave oven and additional storage.

To ensure the scullery doesn't detract from the main kitchen visually, cherry display cabinetry is positioned opposite the entrance. This cabinetry displays glassware and various food items, such as pasta in jars. It also accommodates a collection of small European appliances, which contribute to the overall feel that this is indeed a chef's kitchen.

Designer: Keith Sheedy, Focal Kitchens

Kitchen manufacturer: Focal Kitchens

Cabinetry: Cherry veneers and two-pack satin polyurethane finish

Countertops: Corian on island; textured stainless steel on cooktop area and white Carrara marble in pantry

Flooring: Polished wood

Backsplash: Glass

Oven, hob, ventilation and dishwasher: Gaggenau

Refrigerator: Jenn-Air in kitchen; Liebherr in pantry

Photography by Andrew Ashton

These pages: The scullery is tucked behind the cooking center. This room features similar display cabinetry and incorporates a second food preparation area with a sink and plenty of storage.

Bathrooms

The bathroom has traditionally been considered the 'private', more conservative realm of the home. Yet, as you'll see from this collection of bathroom projects, the transformations taking place in this room are similar to those that have redefined our kitchens.

We no longer want our bathrooms to be simply functional. We want them to be places where we can relax and unwind – with an enjoyable atmosphere and the ambiance of a spa.

So, what are some of the other key aspects to consider when you're planning your new bathroom?

Size and number

The importance we're placing on bathrooms in our homes is highlighted by the fact that they've steadily increased in size and number. For example, it's not unusual these days to have bathrooms associated with all the bedrooms in a home.

As well as the master bathroom, there may be guest bathrooms, and bathrooms designed specifically for the children. Add to that one or more half bathrooms or powder rooms, and it's not unusual for a home to have four, five or six bathrooms.

When it comes to creating a sense of luxury, size is a contributing factor. The desire to have a separate shower and tub also adds to the need for more space. Homeowners who remodel often increase the available space by incorporating the area originally allocated to a separate toilet, or by including space from adjacent storage cupboards or a small bedroom.

However, be aware that major changes to the positioning of plumbing in a remodeling project can be a costly exercise.

Suite dreams

Just as we now consider the kitchen as one element in a group of connected spaces, we're no longer looking at bathrooms in isolation.

If you have the space, you may want to consider integrating your bathroom into the master suite, creating a self-contained area, clearly segregated from other areas of the home.

Although the master bathroom and master bedroom are the two basic components of the suite, you can also include a walk-in closet, sitting area, home office, home gym, secondary laundry room, and even a morning kitchen.

More than just a pretty face

Your bathroom is very much the wet area of your home and needs to cope with potential splashes and spills from baths and sinks, wet footprints,

steam and condensation; which is why impervious materials, such as glazed tiles and porcelain fittings have been traditionally chosen for bathrooms.

But it's not just what's on the surface that's important. The construction of walls and floors, and the use of quality sealers will all play a part in preventing unseen damage that seeping water can cause. This is critical in shower areas, which can cause major problems if not properly built.

Never scrimp on waterproofing, and always use expert installers. Install a good quality extraction system to remove steam and condensation quickly and prevent long-term damage.

Let there be light

When bathrooms were built purely for bathing, they were often tucked away in small, dark areas of a home. These were not intended to be places to linger.

If you've experienced a bright and airy bathroom, which picks up sunlight in the morning or evening, you'll know what a difference that can make to the start or end of your day.

Try to consider how you can introduce natural light into your new bathroom while maintaining privacy from neighboring properties. Careful space planning and the use of translucent materials can overcome these two apparently conflicting requirements.

Fixtures and fittings

The basic components you need for your bathroom are the tub, shower enclosure, sink, faucets and showerhead, toilet and vanity unit or some other storage system. You may also add a bidet, make-up area, steam shower and sitting area.

Your final selection may be a compromise depending on how much space you have, the look you want to achieve and your budget.

Consult an expert

Designing a bathroom may seem to be a simpler exercise than designing a kitchen, but it's still possible to make expensive mistakes. Always talk to an expert.

Our featured bathroom projects allow you to identify looks, fittings and fixtures that you would like to have in your own new bathroom. And a good bathroom designer will find this an invaluable starting point for creating a bathroom in which you can relax and pamper yourself at any time of the day or night.

5

Bathtubs as centerpieces

"A tub makes a wonderful design focal point in a bathroom. It's an element that lends itself to creative placement and composition."

John Battle, architect, Battle Associates

Center of attention

With its 'womb-like' tub area, this bathroom provides a protective
haven with a magnificent view

Architect: John Battle, AIA, Battle Associates (Boston, MA)
Interior designer: Katz Studios
Builder: Kyle Van Winkle
Bathtub: Vintage cast iron by Kohler
Vanity: Waterworks
Basin: Kohler
Faucets and shower fittings: Etoile from Waterworks
Shower stall: Glass blocks from Pittsburgh Corning
Tiles: Custom
Windows: Ricketson custom mahogany
Lighting: Lightolier; Flos

Photography by Kallan MacLeod

Preceding pages: Placed beneath a low, curved ceiling, the tub area is a focal point of this guest bathroom designed by architect, John Battle, from Battle Associates.

Facing page: Framing the view, the customized mahogany window behind the tub has a central panel that opens inwards. The blue-and-white checkerboard tiles around the tub were selected by the owners.

Left: The use of stained wood siding was inspired by traditional New England cottages. Suspended track lighting illuminates the vanity. Glass blocks form the shower enclosure.

Below: A half wall of glass blocks screens the toilet.

Relaxing in the tub is a rare luxury for many of us. But with the spectacular view on offer from this bathroom, a long, hot soak is time well spent.

When architect John Battle proposed a guest bathroom design that would stand out from the norm, the owners of this New England home happily gave him creative carte blanche.

"One of the bonuses with this house was its secluded waterfront outlook, which made it possible to put windows on three sides of the space without the usual privacy concerns," he says.

The bathroom features a shower and vanity along one side, with a toilet and dresser on the opposite wall. At the far end of the space sits the focal point of the bathroom – the tub. Set into a tiled surround, it is framed by an arched ceiling finished in white-stained wood siding.

"The room's layout is anchored around this womb-like tub area," says Battle. "Its curved ceiling, driven by the slope of the roof, adds a very magical feel."

The custom-designed, arched mahogany window behind the tub provides a visual counterpoint to the white walls and furniture, and blends in with the dark wood floor. Its central panel is hinged on one side, allowing it to open inwards.

To emphasize the light-filled nature of the space, and add a contemporary element to the design, Battle incorporated glass blocks into the shower stall, and a half-height wall to screen the toilet.

"The blocks are a fun juxtaposition to the traditionally inspired siding and furniture," he says. "They also give the room a jewel-like quality."

Sound of the sea

Like a large, spiral shell, this free-formed spa bath
lies within a sculpted, fused-glass screen

Left: The owners' collection of contemporary glass sculpture and Native American artworks inspired the eclectic design of this bathroom.

Below: Hand-made fused-glass screens add a translucent, watery look to the bathroom.

Art is a passion for many people, so it's not surprising to see homes filled with treasured collections. For the owners of this home, that passion extends to the master suite, where they can literally surround themselves with sculptural forms that make a strong architectural statement.

Designed by architect Jim Olson, the bathroom reflects the interior design theme of the rest of the condominium. This has been heavily influenced by the waterfront location and the owners' collection of contemporary art and glass, and traditional American Indian art works.

Sculpted fused-glass screens, similar to those used elsewhere in the house, surround a raised tub – the centerpiece of the room. Fused-glass screens also form the exterior of the stand-alone shower.

Below: The tub is lined with stainless steel - a smooth surface reminiscent of a shell interior.

Right: The interior of the shower enclosure is lined with smooth glass for easy maintenance.

Facing page: To enhance the watery feel of the bathroom, the fused-glass shower screen is curved in a spiral shape. The shower is entered from the opening at the right of this picture. Stainless steel clips secure the overlapping glass panels.

"The fused-glass adds a flowing, watery element to the room," says Olson. "The sense of connection with the sea is further enhanced by the way the shower screen curves in a spiral shape, which provides privacy for the owners, yet still allows the light to penetrate."

Similarly, the screen behind the tub covers a window, which eliminates the need for a blind, but still allows light to filter through.

Olson says the tub is designed to resemble a large shell. Alternating stripes of limestone and concrete contribute to the spiral effect at its base. Limestone also forms the tub surround, while the stainless steel lining echoes the smooth interior of a shell. A stainless steel railing follows the curve of the glass screen.

"The underwater effect is further enhanced by the concrete floor," says Olson. "This has a slight muddy look, not unlike the bottom of the sea."

In keeping with the organic nature of the interior and its light, contemporary feel, matching his–and–hers vanities feature white oak cabinetry and limestone countertops.

Left: Glazed ceiling panels and fused-glass wall panels behind the bed continue the watery feel in the master suite. Cantilevered shelving on the bed head adds to the floating effect.

Legend for plan: 1 shower enclosure, 2 master bedroom, 3 closets and changing area, 4 bathtub, 5 steam room.

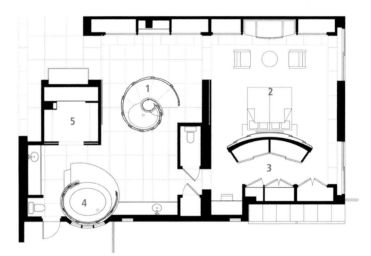

Interior architect: Olson Sundberg Kundig Allen Architects (Seattle, WA); lead architect: Jim Olson, FAIA; project managers: Kelly Brooks, Elizabeth Conklin, Jim Conti

Interior design and furnishings: Lead designer: Jim Olson; project manager: Debbie Kennedy

Builder: Krekow Jennings

Fused-glass walls: Peter David Studios

Flooring: Custom precast concrete from Dogpaw Design

Wallcoverings: Venetian plaster from Legacy Company

Lighting: Alinea

Window treatments: Mecho Shades

Bathtub: Custom design in stainless steel, precast concrete and limestone from Diamond Spas

Vanity cabinetry: Limestone and white oak from Krekow Jennings

Basin: Kohler

Faucets: Dornbracht

Photography by Tim Maloney

Bathing beauty

Timeless materials and a simple, contemporary design
create a warm, inviting feel in this master bathroom

Facing page and left: Architect William Harrison married classic materials with an updated design in this master bathroom of a new Georgian-style home.

Below: Tiled in marble, the spacious shower has sandblasted-glass walls which ensure privacy and lend a light, airy feel to the space.

The increasingly popular concept of the bathroom as a relaxing, spa-like retreat has seen the tub pushed firmly into the spotlight.

While the conventional positioning of the tub would be on a perimeter wall, the owners of this master bath acted on the suggestion of architect William Harrison, placing it in the center of the room.

Set beneath a chandelier hanging from the vaulted, tent-like ceiling, the tub is set into a marble surround, anchored at each corner by a square pedestal.

"While the tub floats in the middle of the room, the pedestals give it a classical, substantial feel," says Harrison.

Contrasting with the pale marble floor, tub surround and vanity top, mahogany wall paneling adds a sense of warmth and richness to the space.

"We intentionally kept the paneling detail simple," he says. "It has classical elements, such as a base and cornice, but is otherwise stripped back to clean, flush finishes that create a contemporary look."

This idea is carried through the entire room, where timeless materials are paired with a simple, sleek design. Harrison says this makes the space feel more like a comfortable room than a functional bathroom.

Positioned symmetrically at either end of the tub, the shower stall and toilet cubicle feature sand-blasted glass walls. As well as providing privacy, these add light and a sense of volume to the room.

Below: A mirrored dressing table occupies the window bay to the left of the tub.

Right: "Placed in the center of the room, the raised tub adds a sense of scale to the space," says architect William Harrison. "Marble pedestals on each corner of the surround give it a classical, substantial feel."

Architect: William Harrison, AIA, and John Albanese, Harrison Design Associates (Atlanta, GA)

Interior designer: Dilger/Gibson

Builder: Jim Roberts, J Roberts Inc

Bathtub: Infinity II Aquatic from Hughes Supply

Vanity top, floor and tiles: Botticino Fiorito marble from Marble Creations

Cabinetry: Mahogany

Basin, toilet, bidet: Kohler from Apex Supply Co

Faucets: Monarch lav set from Paul Decorative

Shower fittings: Aktiva from Apex Supply Co

Lighting and ventilation: Georgia Lighting

Window treatments: Weathershield mahogany shutters

Photography by John Umberger

Weekend escape

With its slipper tub and spectacular view, this master
suite is the perfect retreat for its owners

Architect: Erica Broberg Architect, AIA (East Hampton, NY)
Builder: Peter Joyce Contracting
Bath: Kohler
Faucets: Alan Court & Associates
Shower fittings: Home Expo
Tiles: Limestone from Alan Court & Associates
Toilet: Kohler
Lighting: Home Expo
Ventilation: Nutone fan
Window treatments: Andersen Windows and Doors

Photography by Kallan MacLeod

Summer houses frequently offer a luxury not always available in city residences – space. And for many homeowners, the ultimate luxury is a spacious bathroom that provides a place to unwind and relax in peaceful surroundings, preferably with a view.

Architect Erica Broberg says creating a master suite that is also a private retreat is a priority for many people who own a vacation home.

"For the owners of this renovated waterfront cottage, the bathroom is the nicest room in the house. Its central position not only affords the best view of the harbor and the twinkling lights at night, it also captures the sun during the day."

The bathroom features another essential element for a retreat – a large tub. Broberg says a soaking tub or spa bath is a priority for such master suites, with the style of the tub determining a room's overall look.

"In this instance, a slipper tub sets the tone. But while it has a traditional feel, it is also a pared-down look. There is a clean-lined simplicity that has been reinforced in the design of the cabinetry."

The drawers in the painted wood cabinetry are flush, but the doors match the beadboard wainscoting. Broberg says that although the entire second floor of the cottage is new, the architecture – both outside and in – reflects a traditional Hamptons' influence.

"The beadboard wainscoting, painted in a warm white shade, is part of that language of the beach," she says. "So, too, is the gabled roofline, which adds to the sense of space in the bathroom and allows for a small high window above the tub. I call this a happy detail. It draws the eye upwards to the blue of the sky."

Simplicity is also a feature of the tiled flooring. Limestone tiles have been laid on the diagonal – to avoid a hotel look. A patterned inlay reflects the gold and green colors of the nearby dunes.

A spacious corner shower with a frameless glass door reinforces the streamlined look.

Facing page and above left: Designed as a parents' retreat, this bathroom in a renovated vacation cottage features a large slipper tub. The position of the tub beside the window ensures bathers can enjoy an uninterrupted view of the harbor.

Above: Limestone tiles are a feature of both the flooring and the shower, which has built-in shelving for ease of use. The flooring tiles are laid on the diagonal and incorporate a patterned inlay. Architect Erica Broberg says the beadboard detailing on the cabinetry doors is similar to the wainscoting throughout the house, and is a traditional beach house feature.

6
Master suites

"Incorporating a bedroom-and-bathroom suite into your home allows you to create a very personal environment that intimately fits your way of living."

Eric McClelland, interior designer, Fleur De Lis Interior Design

All together

This design allows the bathroom, bedroom, study and sitting areas to share an open-plan space

Preceding pages: Cedar cabinetry provides a unifying element. The earth material palette is reinforced by the use of concrete block above the fireplace.

Left: A large Plexiglas and stainless steel partition shields the vanities from the rest of the bedroom area.

Below: A hammered copper coffee table and leather chairs contribute to the interior's warm, earthy tones.

Sometimes an area of a family home is set aside as a grown-ups' sanctuary. Achieving a multipurpose master suite that leaves the kids behind when the door is closed requires a clever use of materials and partitioning.

This project combines several distinct uses into a 1600sq ft pavilion set apart from the home's central living area. The parents needed a self-contained space, but at the same time wanted to retain the lake views from throughout the pavilion, says interior designer Eric McClelland.

"By the strategic use of partitioning, creating an open-plan design, almost every spot has views out to the lake," says McClelland. "Various forms of partitioning have been created that work both as decor features and points of division."

Perhaps the most dramatic divide separates the central bedroom space from the bathtub and vanities. This takes

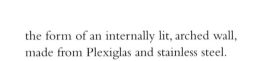

the form of an internally lit, arched wall, made from Plexiglas and stainless steel.

On another side, a millwork bedhead separates the sleeping area from the shower. Built out of Canadian cedar, with an inlaid sandblasted pine design element, the headboard millwork also fulfills the role of providing cabinetry for the shower area.

Elsewhere in the central area, couches are set back-to-back to provide a subtle division of use. On one side of the couches lies the lounge area, on the other is a small viewing area looking out onto the lake.

In practical terms, the type of flooring differentiates the wet areas from the dry. Azulon limestone used on the vanity

tops is repeated on the floors of the bath and shower areas. In the study and sleeping areas, the floors are Jatoba – a Brazilian mahogany.

"Although the pavilion is large, it required careful thought to ensure disparate areas achieved individual identity and also worked well together," McClelland says. "A warm material palette was key to providing harmony in this area. Natural materials, like leather, copper and cedar, all combine to give the interior a Zen-like material ambiance."

The pavilion's other unifying element is the scenery itself, with the layout keeping it in view at every turn – from bed to bath.

Facing page: The border on the curtain in the study was chosen to blend with the cedar cabinets.

Left: Limestone and glass surfaces are used on the divide between shower and study. Individual lamp styles help to define each area.

Below: This master suite by Eric McClelland and Peter Lunney of Fleur De Lis Interior Design uses a variety of elements to differentiate uses within an open-plan pavilion. At the pavilion entrance, a sheet of frosted glass acts as a hanging design feature, shielding the bathroom from the entranceway.

Architect: Murakami Design (Toronto, Canada)

Interior designer: Eric McClelland, ARIDO, NCIDQ, Peter Lunney, ARIDO, NCIDQ, Fleur De Lis Interior Design

Main contractor: Tamarak North Construction

Floor: Azulon limestone from Stone Tile, Jatoba Brazilian hardwood from Tamarak North Construction

Windows: Custom Spanish oak from Tradewood Industries

Bathtub: Maax-Calla VI

Vanity: Cedar with limestone countertop from Z+D Finishes

Cabinetry: Custom cedar from Z+D Finishes

Faucets: Richelieu in stainless steel

Basin: Italian white glass from Taps, Bath and Tile Centre

Shower: Genesis 55 from Wholesale Bathroom Centre

Bathtub surround: Lagos Blue sandstone from Tamarak North Construction

Lighting: Eurolite, Eureka

Window treatments: Two-tone linen

Photography by Elaine Kilburn

Ease into the day

An unusual linear layout creates a relaxing design for
this master bathroom suite

Left: Interior designer Alan Boyd contributed to the decor of this master suite by including subtle design elements, such as the alabaster chandelier seen reflected in the mirror above the washbasin.

Below: The suite by is broken up linearly into a series of five intimate spaces.

Getting up weekday mornings is a chore many of us do not look forward to. However, waking up to the thought of having your very own suite of rooms in which to prepare for the day ahead would go a long way to easing the burden.

The owners of this home lead busy lives. Often, the only time they get to pamper themselves is in the morning, says Philip Liederbach of Liederbach & Graham Architects.

"Mornings can be very jarring, and this master bedroom suite creates a very pleasant way to slip oneself into the day," he says.

"Rather than design one large space, we divided the master suite into a linear series of rooms," says Liederbach.

"The bathroom occupies a space in the sunnier, south side of the home, with large windows flooding each room with morning light."

Interior French doors open from the bedroom into a compact washroom with twin basins. Beyond this point is a small dressing room-cum-powder room.

"The large built-in dresser in this center room maintains order in the master suite, with numerous custom drawers, including compartments for shavers and hair-dryers, complete with power outlets," says Liederbach.

The relatively compact floor area of the dressing amplifies the dwarfing effect of a 14ft-high ceiling, creating an almost cathedral-like ambiance. From here, a 6ft by 8ft arch leads to the bathing area.

Below: Quality materials have been used extensively throughout this bathroom, including St Marcs limestone for the flooring and Massasgis Jaune limestone on the countertops. The scale of the design relates to the architecture of the rest of the house. The spaces in this suite can be compartmentalized using sliding doors, which sit flush within the entrance arches when open.

Right: Saint Marcs limestone reflects the grandeur of this home. The nickel faucet and hand shower continue the theme introduced by the nickel dressing stool. The hand shower is convenient for rinsing hair and washing the bath after use.

Three alcoves in the bathing area – one at each end of the bathtub and one on the back wall – help break up the shape of this room, creating a more intimate ambiance than one might expect. These alcoves provide convenient areas for candles, or art, such as the statuette above the bath, or the shelf created by the bricked-in arch.

"Although the combined length of the rooms is approximately 40ft, spacial character defines each area, while contributing to the overall intimate aesthetic," says Liederbach.

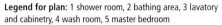

Legend for plan: 1 shower room, 2 bathing area, 3 lavatory and cabinetry, 4 wash room, 5 master bedroom

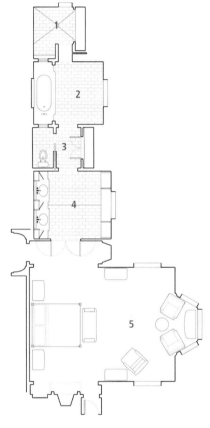

Architect: Principal architect: Philip Liederbach; project architect: Erica Weeder, both from Liederbach & Graham Architects (Chicago, IL)

Interior designer: Alan Boyd, Alan Boyd Inc

Main contractor: Dennis Smalley Builders

Bed: Pranich & Associates

Cabinets: Wilmot Woodworks

Lighting: Besselink, Jones & Milne

Bathtub: Waterworks

Faucets: Chicago Faucets and Waterworks

Basin: Kohler

Vanity tops: Massasgis Jaune limestone

Flooring: St Marcs limestone

Photography by John Umberger

Nothing to hide

Inspired by the Zen-like quality of Asian architecture, this remodeled master suite is spacious, open and filled with light

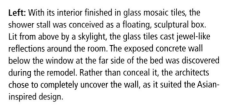

Left: With its interior finished in glass mosaic tiles, the shower stall was conceived as a floating, sculptural box. Lit from above by a skylight, the glass tiles cast jewel-like reflections around the room. The exposed concrete wall below the window at the far side of the bed was discovered during the remodel. Rather than conceal it, the architects chose to completely uncover the wall, as it suited the Asian-inspired design.

Below: Topped with honed gray CaesarStone, the quarter-sawn cherry vanity unit was designed to float above the bamboo floor.

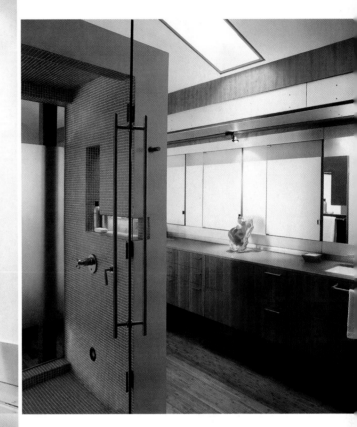

Open plan is a term more frequently applied to a living room than a master bathroom suite. But the idea of having an all-in-one sleeping, relaxing and bathing space is becoming popular.

When it came to remodeling the master suite of their house, owners Aura and Fred Kuperberg chose the most radical of three schemes proposed by Jose Fontiveros and Mariana Boctor of Sintesi Design.

Their design transformed the previously cramped, compartmentalized space into a large, open-plan room with the bathroom and bedroom zones visually separated by a glazed, floating shower box.

"The shower is normally pushed into the corner of the bathroom," says Fontiveros. "We wanted to make it a feature by placing it in the center of the room."

Not simply a functional element, the shower was also conceived as a sculptural feature. With the walls raised slightly off the ground, the shower box appears to float just above the bamboo floor.

A void in the top opens to a skylight above, allowing the sun to reflect off the glass tiles that line the interior walls of the shower.

The four exterior sides are finished in a range of materials, including clear and frosted glass and Masonite, with cherry

Facing page: An L-shaped, glazed cutout adds visual interest to the shower stall and provides a shelf for soap and shampoo.

Left: Clean lines and warm materials give this remodeled master suite an inviting, spacious feel. At the far end of the vanity unit is the toilet cubicle.

Below: The vanity unit continues along the wall and runs behind the bed to form the night stand. A TV screen on an automated lift is recessed into the foot of the bed.

wood for the linen cabinet.

"We tried to include some less expensive materials, like the lacquered Masonite, to balance out the cost of more expensive finishes, such as the glass mosaic tiles," says Boctor.

The bathroom end of the suite features a separate toilet with an etched-glass wall. Adjacent to this is the cherry

Left: Skylights in the ceiling and French doors opening onto the courtyard bring natural light into the room by day. A palette of neutral tones accentuates the light, open feel.

Below: Located in a Japanese-inspired, louvered annex, the bath overlooks the private garden, and is protected from the elements by glass panels inset into the framework.

vanity unit which acts as a connecting element, extending along the entire length of the suite to form the night stand behind the bed.

"Like the shower and bed, the vanity is raised off the floor to reinforce the sense of space, creating a clean, minimalist look," says Boctor. "Continuing the vanity along the wall helped tie everything together."

Insufficient storage space was a major shortcoming of the original bathroom design.

To counter this, Boctor and Fontiveros had eight discreet storage units fitted into the wall above the vanity top. At the bed end of the room, these four-inch-deep cavities house racks for ties and jewelry. Behind the vanity mirror, they provide storage for toiletries.

Architects: Jose Fontiveros and Mariana Boctor, Sintesi Design (Santa Monica, CA)

Design team: Maria Venegas, Juan Calaf, John Erskine, Ben Gramann and Sachiko Sueki

Interior design: Kathleen Greenberg and Erica Steenstra

Builder: Sintesi Design

Vanity: Quarter-sawn cherry wood with CaesarStone countertop

Cabinetry and other joinery: Miguel Tejeras of Marmig Custom Cabinets

Basin, toilet: Kohler

Bathtub: Dornbracht

Faucets: Dornbracht metal satin

Shower stall: AGL Glass Specialties

Tiles: Glass mosaic tiles in Bottle Glass from Walker Zanger

Flooring: Pre-finished bamboo from JS Hardwood

Hot water systems: American Appliances from Ezequiel Plumbing

Lighting: Juno from Villegas Electric

Windows: Douglas fir from Master Custom Doors & Windows

Glasswork: Amber acid-etch mirror from Pulp Studio Glass

Photography by Kallan MacLeod

Private retreat

This spacious master suite not only provides separate his-and-hers facilities, it's also an undisturbed sanctuary for the owners

Facing page: The bathtub is positioned on an axis that aligns the bathroom doors and windows. Flush cabinetry, either side of the ante room leading to the bathroom, enhances the contemporary feel of the space.

Below: Mirrored closet doors line the passage to the master suite.

Below right: Doors feature rice-paper glass, which provides privacy while still allowing light to filter through to the ante room. The second toilet room, which has a sandblasted glass door, is situated in the corner near the vanity dressing table.

On the surface, it might seem that empty-nesters no longer need a place to escape the noise and bustle of a busy household. But factor in family visits, and there's often a need for grandparents to take time out.

The owners of this house established their own private sanctuary – a master suite that's complete with separate his-and-hers facilities, an office space and a large sitting area.

The suite was part of a major remodeling project by interior designer Josh Behr and architect-builders Michael Menn and Andy Poticha. The project included combining and enlarging two bathrooms and extending the master bedroom by six feet.

To enhance the sense of separation, the bedroom is reached via a passage lined with mirrored closets. Both the study and bathroom open from this hallway, which features rice-paper glass skylights that match the glass of the bathroom doors. The bathroom has its own ante room, also lined with cabinetry.

Menn says the owners wanted to share some spaces in the suite, but also have individual facilities. This was achieved by creating separate vanity areas and toilet rooms within the overall bathroom space.

"Creating a very open and airy environment was important," Menn says. "Two skylights and large windows ensure there is plenty of natural light."

The centerpiece of the room is a large tub, positioned beneath the windows on an axis aligning the entrance. Glass-walled spaces on either side of the tub accommodate the shower and the husband's toilet room, which incorporates a urinal. The other toilet room is on the opposite wall.

"The lower half of each glass wall is sandblasted, which provides privacy while still letting in light," says Menn. "The glass also enhances the contemporary feel of the space."

Behr says the bathroom fit-out was designed to reflect the eclectic nature of the rest of the house.

"There is a distinct Art Deco feel about the interior," he says. "The owners also have an extensive art collection, which includes both contemporary and Asian works."

Below: Bathroom mirrors are framed by backlit glass panels with an embedded copper fabric. The walls also feature copper – the metallic paint has a faux finish.

Right: Furnishings combine contemporary and antique items, enhancing the eclectic look of the bathroom. The glass-walled room beyond the tub accommodates a toilet and urinal.

Behr says the original interior of the 20-year-old house was painted white.

"We wanted to bring in more color, to warm the spaces up and make them a little friendlier," he says. "The color palette of terra cotta tones was inspired by the art collection."

In keeping with the desire to create a sanctuary, the bathroom includes furniture – an antique-style Chinese table and vase sit alongside a contemporary Italian bench seat. And modern sculpture on one side of the room is contrasted by a traditional Asian statue on the opposite side.

"It was important to balance the very eclectic mix of furniture and objets d'art," says Behr.

Using natural materials helps achieve this visual balance.

The floor features light-colored limestone, while the vanity tops are a rich granite in tones of copper and burgundy. Glass tiles around the tub and in the shower provide reflective surfaces, retaining the contemporary feel.

Interior designer: Behr Design Studio (Chicago, IL)

Main contractor: Design Construction Concepts, AIA, NAHB

Windows: Pella Architectural Series

Rice-paper glass: Sumi Glass

Blinds: Kravet Fabrics from Interior Dynamics

Bedroom carpet: Peerless Rug

Bedroom furniture: Donghia Fabrics from Interior Dynamics

Flooring tiles: Imperial Gold limestone

Wall tiles: Veneto Glass Tiles

Vanity: Custom from Nu-Trend Cabinet Co

Vanity tops: Rosso Damasco marble from Damar Stone

Basin: Kohler Caxton

Basin faucets: Grohe in satin nickel

Bathtub: Kohler

Bathtub faucet: Vola in satin nickel

Shower fittings: Grohe body sprays, rain dome shower head and hand-held shower

Shower steam unit: Mister Steam

Toilet, urinal and bidet: Toto

Lighting: Juno Recess

Ventilation: Broan

Photography by Mike Kaskel

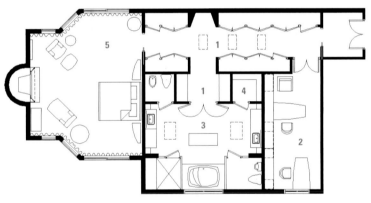

Matching his-and-hers vanity units are lacquered in a warm chocolate brown.

"Balancing light and dark, hard and soft, and warm and cool elements provides a continuity with the rest of the house interior," says Behr.

Functionality was another priority for the bathroom. The walk-in shower has no sill, allowing easy access. Lighting is also positioned to provide the best light for shaving or applying make-up. And a large, corner closet provides plenty of accessible space for towel storage.

Legend for plan: 1 walk-through closets, 2 office with two desks, 3 bathroom, 4 linen closet, 5 main bedroom.

Right: The walk-in steam shower, designed for easy access, incorporates gold glass tiles, multiple shower heads and a bench seat.

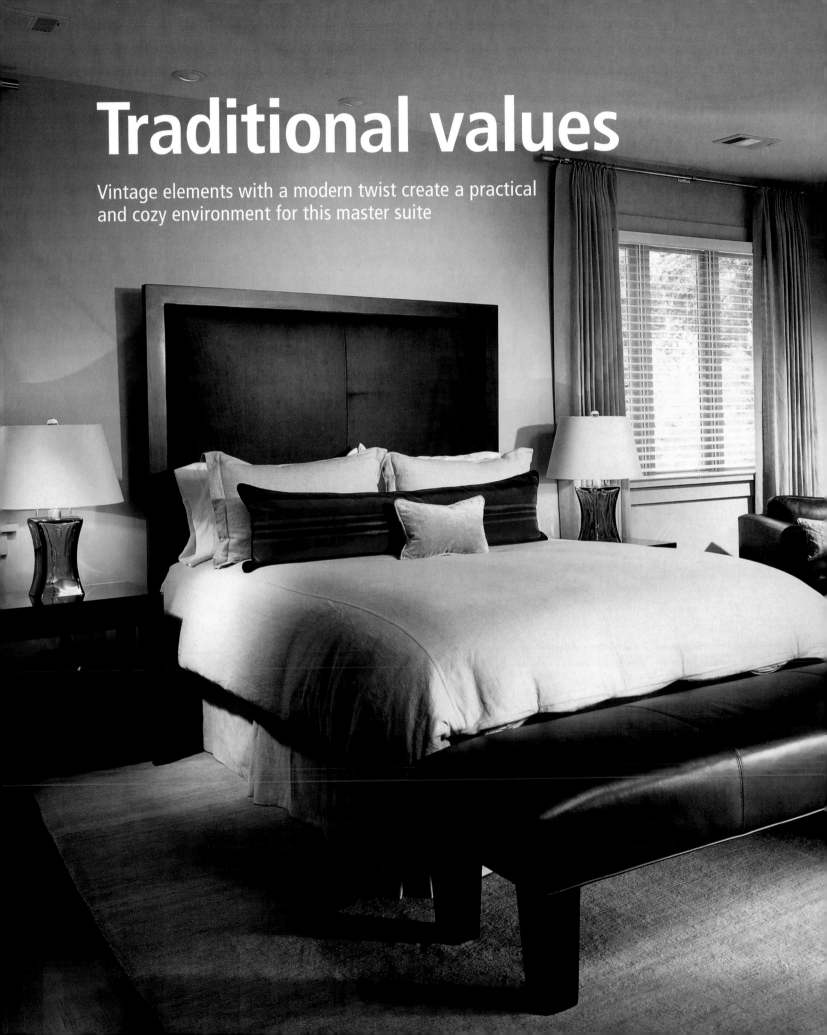

Traditional values

Vintage elements with a modern twist create a practical and cozy environment for this master suite

Left: The bedroom of this master suite, by designers Eric Rothman and Jenny Nelson, interprets old-world architecture with some sophisticated, modern touches.

Below: Painting the walls and window trims a uniform matt color draws attention to the view and art, while emphasizing the clean lines of this design. Three opaque windows, to the left of the vanity, provide a multiple source of light, which creates a softer ambiance. Mounting the faucets and spout on the wall keeps the countertop clean and uncluttered.

Historical architectural features, such as wide baseboards, geometric symmetry, and the use of solid materials including stone, give a space a sense of strength and longevity. Paired with contemporary highlights and a well thought-out floor plan, the result can be an enticing space to spend time in.

The owner's requirements for this project were to create a simple space that feels inviting and is easy to maintain, says designer Eric Rothman of design-and-build company HammerSmith.

"There is something modern about this design, but I wouldn't describe it as contemporary, " says Rothman. "It's more like a reinterpretation of Victorian architecture, influenced by minimalism, but with more warmth."

A dark, coffee bean oak floor has an antique quality. This flooring is accentuated by 8in baseboards that create a simple transition between the floor and the walls.

"There is a carved-out quality to these rooms, which gives this design an almost sculptural quality," says Rothman.

Oak flooring continues in the bathroom and contrasts with the freestanding cherry cabinetry.

Legend for plan: 1 master bedroom, 2 study, 3 wardrobe, 4 opaque windows, 5 tub, 6 tiled feature wall and basins, 7 shower stall, 8 lavatory

Right: A frameless glass shower enclosure helps make this room appear larger than it actually is. Keeping the design clean and simple maintains the orderly aesthetic of the space.

Facing page: Built-in cubbyholes above the tub contribute to the carved, sculptural quality of the suite.

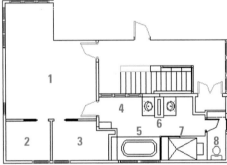

"You have to be careful when combining wood grains. But the cherry complements the oak, creating a smooth transition between the wood to the freestanding feature wall," says Rothman.

Tiling the wall in Pewter fossil stone adds multiple levels of interest, contributing to the sculptured aesthetic of this space.

"The stone tiles look clean and simple from a distance, but the detailing, visible up-close, creates interest and intrigue," says Rothman.

The top ledge of the wall provides a place to put toothbrushes and other bathroom accessories, keeping the basin areas clean and uncluttered. Concrete countertops accentuate the geometric simplicity of this design.

The same tiling is used around the bath and shower stall.

Enclosing the shower with clear glazing allows the tiles to act as an architectural link with the walls, and tub surround. The transparency of the glass contributes to the overall feeling of space.

A white tub contrasts with the darker tones of the wood grains on the floor and cabinetry, making it stand out as a design feature.

"We've created structure, then deliberately broken it by placing a curved tub amongst the angles. This makes it look placed, so the space takes on a more human feeling," says Rothman.

Design team: Eric Rothman and Jenny Nelson, NKBA, NARI, HBA, HammerSmith (Decatur, GA)

Main contractor: HammerSmith

Bathtub: Lefroy Brooks XO Zen from Apex Supply

Vanity countertop: Concrete Seal Grey from J Aron Cast Stone

Cabinetry: Custom, in cherry

Basin: Ovalyn Undermount from American Standard

Faucets: Concinnity Malmo, in satin nickel

Shower fittings: Concinnity Apex

Flooring: Oak from Cherokee Floors

Tiles: Honed Pewter Fossil Stone from Natural Stone

Lighting: LBL from Illuminations

Ventilation: Panasonic from Georgia Lighting

Photography by John Umberger

7

Links to the outdoors

"Indoor-outdoor flow should be about more than doors opening out to a patio. You can link your interior with nature through skylights, glass walls, natural materials and by stepping a space down into the garden."

Sue Lanier, architect, Lubowicki Lanier Architecture

Part of the scenery

The design of this suite lets nature in at every opportunity, while from the outside appearing at one with its garden environment

Preceding pages: This suite by Lubowicki Lanier Architecture is designed to feel at one with the outdoors. Frosted glass doors slide out from shower walls for privacy.

Facing page: Light filters under the eaves onto minimalist forms, giving the roof a floating appearance.

This page: The internal space is defined by several white walls. The custom basin is by design consultant Susan Stringfellow.

An effective way for a house to connect with the outdoors is by creating rooms that appear to sit amongst the scenery, rather than simply look out on it.

This was the aim of architect Sue Lanier and design consultant Susan Stringfellow when they created this light and airy bedroom suite, part of a contemporary extension to a 1920s cottage.

"The extension comprises a dining area, sun room and, lastly, the bedroom suite, which steps down to the same level as the garden," says Lanier.

Several elements contribute to the suite's easy connection with the outdoors.

"As well as floor-to-ceiling windows and skylights, the 'pulled-apart' nature of the design allows glimpses of sky from strip windows under the eaves – giving the roof a floating appearance," says Lanier. "Looking down into the suite from the entry stairs, the design elements appear to scale down towards the garden. This culminates in a fireplace, surrounded by glass, at the end of the bedroom."

Nestled at ground level, from outside, the low bedroom concrete wall could be taken for a garden wall. This is intended to give the suite the look of a garden feature, rather than an imposing structure.

"From the outside, one can view past the eaves to the Douglas fir rafters that comprise the ceiling," says Lanier.

The choice of materials gives the bedroom another strong connection with the outdoors. Simple, natural surfaces include the Douglas fir ceiling rafters, concrete walls, and limestone tile floors. Glass and stainless steel provide contrasting elements.

Natural colors were also important to the design. The roof's weathered metal hues can be seen as it wraps in under the suite's eaves. A wash was applied to the Douglas fir to tone down its bright orange hues, in keeping with an overall palette of muted gray tones. Warm aggregate tones were introduced to the concrete, to pick up the hues of the limestone tiles. These tiles are slightly textured and run throughout the space, including the shower stall.

This page: There are no curtains in this bedroom suite. An element of privacy is achieved by the internal walls, which form the shower area.

Facing page: Smooth surfaces are contrasted with the textured surface of the poured-in-place concrete wall.

Everything about the design is pared back. Personal care items are tucked out of sight. The bed is low and minimalist, and the doors to the outside have no threshold.

"The suite has an uncluttered, monastic feel," says Stringfellow. "It's all about space, light and materials – concrete, wood and limestone."

Architect: Lubowicki Lanier Architecture (Los Angeles, CA)

Design consultant: Susan Stringfellow

Interior furnishings: Kay Kollar Design

Builder: Alexander Construction

Cabinetry: Custom Douglas fir, vertical grain, clear finish

Basin: Custom in brushed stainless steel from Metalmorphosis

Faucets: Vola in chrome

Shower fittings: Vola, Speakman

Shower stall: Custom

Flooring: Buxy Gris limestone from Eurostone Concepts

Toilet: Cadet in white by American Standard

Lighting: Capri from Fire

Accessories: Linens by Nancy Stanley

Photography by Tim Maloney

Wild frontier

Granite blocks hewn into bathtubs and sinks
reflect the rugged alpine wilderness outside

Facing page: Windows above the tub and shower look out to the magnificent scenery. Construction details are the same outside and in the house.

Left: The handbasin in the master bathroom was hewn from a single block of granite, found abandoned on a ranch in the same state. Douglas fir paneling and metal window frames are the other materials used in the room.

It seems perfectly understandable – when a house is built among spectacular surroundings – to want to enjoy the views from both inside and outdoors.

When Walker Warner Architects was asked to design a cabin in a valley below craggy mountain peaks, the owners' brief was that the house should not try to compete with the scenery.

"They wanted to feel part of the landscape, both from inside and outside the house and this applied to the bathrooms too," says architect Kathy Scott.

The house is built from salvaged Douglas fir, using a post and beam construction, with panels of the wood covering the walls. This system allowed for large expanses of glass, which assisted the interior and exterior connection.

A strictly limited palette of materials – fir, stone and steel – ensures the space is free of fuss.

Continuing the natural theme, the tub and handbasin are made from granite, reflecting the peaks behind the house. The basin is carved from one block, with the natural face left in its raw state. Only the inner surface is bushed to make it smoother. Because of the weight of the granite, the tub was built from smaller pieces, fitted together to create a sense that it is hewn from a single block.

Architect: Brooks Walker, Kathy Scott, Marshall Schneider, Walker Warner Architects (San Francisco, CA)

Interior designer: Stacy Stone, Stone Interiors

Main contractor: Mark Nolan

Bathtub and basin: Custom granite from Edwin Hamilton Stoneworks

Vanity: Reclaimed Douglas fir

Faucets: Rocky Mountain Hardware from Mission Wood Products

Hot water system: Aquastar from Real Goods

Flooring: Antique heart pine from Urban Developments

Wallcoverings: Reclaimed Douglas fir paneling from The Cascade Joinery

Tiles: Granite tub surround from Edwin Hamilton Stoneworks

Lighting: Galaxy Gas Products from Lehman Hardware

Accessories: Rocky Mountain Hardware

Cabinet hardware: Jefferson Mack Metal

Photography by Cesar Rubio

Opposites attract

Thousands of glass mosaic tiles form an abstract mural that visually contrasts with the tropical planting both in and outside this bathroom

Architect: Ron Radziner, AIA, Marmol Radziner and Associates, (Los Angeles, CA)

Builder: Marmol Radziner and Associates

Faucets: Concinnity

Shower fittings: Concinnity and Dornbracht

Shower stall: Custom frameless enclosure

Tiles: Bisazza, Vitricolor 20 from California Art Tile

Photography by John Ellis

Facing page: The color of the mosaic tiles changes to visually signal each area of the bathroom. For example, in the rectangular bathtub there is a mix of light and dark blue tiles.

Left: A niche in the wall provides a shelf for soap and shampoo. The mosaic tiles on this wall form a geometric step pattern, providing visual contrast to the soft tropical planting below.

In geometry every object can be made identical. In nature no two things are exactly alike. Yet, marry them together in design and each can complement the other.

LA-based architect Ron Radziner played with the idea of combining two opposite forms when designing this bathroom. He installed thousands of tiny square mosaic tiles on the walls and floor, and set them against a natural backdrop.

"It's like an abstract mural, with shapes created in and out, and up and down the walls. The internal garden, between the shower and window, brings the random quality of nature into direct contrast with this geometric design," he says.

To reflect the progress from an interior into an outdoor environment, the tiles gradually change in color. At the bathroom's entrance, they are beige, in the shower and bath they are blue,

and closer the window, the tiles change again, to green. The plain white ceiling provides visual relief.

On the small dividing wall between the garden and shower, light-colored blue tiles signpost where steps drop down to form a deep rectangular bathtub.

A large, double shower door, contains the water in the bathroom's wet area, without shutting out the natural light from the window.

Organic flow

Bathrooms at this island retreat allow guests to
feel part of nature and at one with the scenery

Left: The natural environment outside is emphasized by organic forms inside. Flowing plasterwork in mottled hues gives the bathroom a soft, natural feel.

Below: The view takes center stage at this island lodge designed by architect Ron Stevenson. A deep, two-seater tub provides bathers with a scenic outlook.

For a getaway vacation spot, it makes sense to maximize the natural surroundings from every vantage point. One of the most restful and contemplative places to take in the scenery is from the privacy of your bathroom. The owner of the scenic lodge on this island embraced this idea when considering the design of the bathrooms.

The brief to the designers for Delamore Lodge, was to re-create the feel of the natural environment that lay beyond the windows, says lodge owner and manager Roselyn Barnett-Storey.

"Natural materials are emphasized throughout the bathrooms, and organic forms sculpted into or out from the plastered walls accentuate this," she says. "A large, deep bath beside the window is set up high. With the windows open, the occupant can enjoy uninterrupted views of the scenery."

The bathrooms have an expansive feel, due to the extensive use of windows and an open shower area.

"The shower and bathing area are defined by a textured pebble floor," says the owner. "The pebbles provide a link to the natural environment, and have a pleasing massaging effect underfoot."

Plaster walls and a plaster ceiling in variegated tones have a flowing, organic feel. This look is extended to the molded

plaster bath surround and bath seat.

"The effect is as if the two-seater bath grows out of the building's structure, avoiding sharp lines and angles," says Barnett-Storey. "Even the soap receptacles next to the shower and bath have rounded edges, and are recessed into the plaster."

The vanity's backsplash is simply a raised area of plasterwork. This outlines the basin area without being obtrusive against the wall's texture and tone.

Natural wood, used for the vanity top, further extends the natural theme, while Kohler basins and glass shelving add a contemporary touch.

Architect: Ron Stevenson

Walls: Plasterwork by Rob Barker, Phil Chatfield

Floors: Concrete

Vanity: Elm wood

Basins, faucets and shower rose: Kohler

Photography by Kallan MacLeod

Facing page: Softly contoured basins sit on top of a natural wood countertop, underscoring the room's organic feel.

Above: The open shower area is defined by natural pebble flooring which provides a massaging effect underfoot.

Rustic ambiance

This bathtub takes center stage, amid a backdrop
inspired by nature

Architect: Charles R Stinson, AIA, ASID,
Charles R Stinson Architects (Minnetonka, MN)

Interior designer: Charles R Stinson and the homeowners

Builder: Donald Streeter, Streeter & Associates

Cabinetry: Brad Brandton

Bathtub: Iron Works Tellieur from Kohler

Faucets: Vogt Plumbing

Shower stall: Van Anderson Italian travertine

Wallcoverings: Faux painting from Daniel Otto Painting

Tiles: Tiles Plus

Electrician: Suburban Electric

Lighting: Holly Hunt from Lighting Fixture Supplies

Photography by Kallan MacLeod

If there was ever a room in which to relax and contemplate, far removed from the hustle and bustle of modern life, it would surely be the master bathroom. Which is why natural materials and subtle light effects provide an ideal setting for an indulgent soak in the bathtub.

Architect Charles Stinson was asked to design a bathroom that promoted the feeling of being inside an old stone castle. To create this effect he built a feature wall of oversized stone blocks and set the mortar deep to accentuate the stone's color and texture.

The room's focal point, the large white freestanding bathtub, is set into a black walnut frame. The same wood is used for the shutters covering a window that looks onto large evergreen trees.

During the day, these shutters allow shafts of light to illuminate the area, creating linear patterns on the tiled floor. At night, an entirely different ambiance is achieved by dozens of pinlights positioned on the top of each individual piece of stone. These tiny lights create drama and shadow play across the wall, Stinson says.

Recessed halogens have also been strategically placed in the ceiling. These lights, along with the pin lights, can be controlled from the home's central lighting system.

Designing a bathroom that enhances the cleansing ritual was inspired by the owners' time in Asia, where the act of bathing takes on an almost spiritual dimension, says Stinson.

However, the practicalities of contemporary living are also well catered to in this bathroom. His-and-hers vanities are in the same room as the bathtub.

They are positioned on either side of a short hallway that leads to the toilet and shower.

The travertine tiles covering the shower enclosure create a look which Stinson says is in keeping with the entire bathroom's cave-like atmosphere.

"It's a nice feeling, being inside an enclosed, tactile space, with the crisp, smooth texture of the heated tiles beneath your feet."

Facing page: This freestanding bathtub is set inside a black walnut frame. It is the focal point of a bathroom, in which solid raw materials such as stone and wood create a rustic backdrop.

Above left: His-and-hers vanities in the master bathroom are positioned inside niches on either side of the entrance to a short hallway. The toilet is on the left, the shower on the right.

Above right: The limestone tiles that surround the shower emphasize the feeling of being inside a cave or an old stone castle.

Capture the sky

A window in this bathroom opens onto a small, trellised garden, ushering in sunlight and helping to create a sense of space

Left: Reflected in the mirror of this small bathroom is a planter box enclosed in a trellis. While natural light floods the room, the trellis ensures the owners' privacy is not sacrificed.

Below: The basin was selected for its sculptural appeal. Its wide rim has plenty of room for soap and flannels.

There are few things more revitalizing than taking a shower under the sun or beneath the stars. But welcoming in nature – without compromising privacy – is a challenge when designing a small bathroom that is overlooked by neighboring houses.

In the bathroom featured here, architect Thomas Tow of Tow Francis Architecture + Urban Design has made full use of the natural light that shines through the window. Behind the glass is a custom-built planter box enclosed in a wooden trellis. The trellis is placed upside down so that its slats are positioned upwards. This means anyone using the shower can view the sky but not be seen from the outside, says Tow.

Architect: Thomas Tow, Tow Francis Architecture + Urban Design

Builder: Advance Project Team

Basin: Laufen

Faucets: Bodenschatz

Tiles: Platinum quartzite

Toilet: Laufen

Photography by Tim Nolan

"The trellis screens out the neighbors without compromising the natural light. When the window is open, it makes the bathroom appears much larger than it actually is."

To ensure this small bathroom didn't seem claustrophobic or appear cluttered, a limited palette of natural materials has been used.

"The client wanted the look and atmosphere of a mountain spa. We chose stone tiling for the walls and floor, complemented by wooden framing around the mirrors," Tow says.

The quartzite stone tiles were cut to a size of 12in x 12in. Although stone is a heavy material, the tiles have a silvery green facade that reflects light and adds to the feeling of being in a tropical resort, says Tow.

By placing a mirror above the basin and mirrors along the wall opposite the window, the bathroom appears to double in size.

Behind these mirrors are his-and-hers cabinets. A shelf built into the stone-tiled wall below the cabinets houses the towels.

The basin is a single, sculptural piece that has been mounted onto the wall. The mirrored cabinets and the linen cupboard above the toilet eliminate the need for vanity cabinets below the basin.

"To keep the design simple, every fitting and piece of furniture has a purpose," says Tow.

Separating the shower and toilet is a glass screen, stretching halfway across the shower area.

"No door has been installed because none was required – the glass screen is enough to contain the water inside the shower," he says.

The sunken shower floor is reminiscent of Japanese design and adds a certain exotic appeal.

"Lowering the floor heightens the shower experience. The person using the shower feels utterly enclosed in the space," says Tow.

Above left: Sunlight filters through the trellis outside the bathroom.

Above right: Stone tiles cover the wall and the floor to create the impression of being in a mountain spa. The stone is visually complemented by the wooden mirror frames.

Facing page: A clear glass screen is all that separates the shower and toilet.

8

Colors & materials

"Achieving a harmony of tones and finishes means taking into account their inherent feel; setting off dark with light, rough with smooth, and warm with cold."

Marcus Gleysteen, architect, Gleysteen Design LLC

Preceding pages: Architect Marcus Gleysteen has brought together an eclectic celebration of color, texture, materials and shapes to create this bathroom as a functioning work or art.

Below: The cut of the Babinga African hardwood veneer gives it a lustrous, warm satin finish that contrasts with the cool tilework and stainless steel utilities.

Right: Facing mirrors increase the bathroom's sense of space. The curved lines of the stainless steel corner tub provide contrast with the bathroom's cabinetry and tilework.

Achieving an interior that effectively combines a range of materials and tones takes a delicate touch. As well as finding a balance of color, the warmth of the finishes and even their textures and shapes also need to be addressed to achieve perfect harmony.

For this bathroom, the client wanted to combine colors and materials in such a way as to create a functioning work of art, says architect Marcus Gleysteen.

"Window frames were custom made from steel, along the lines of a Mondrian painting," says Gleysteen. "Their uneven but harmonized proportions are indicative of the make-up of the entire bathroom."

The first step to achieving this delicate balance was to lay out a diverse array of tiles, wood, glass, stainless steel

Balancing act

Disparate tones, textures and materials achieve
a fine aesthetic harmony in this bathroom

Below: For continuity, the stainless steel handles are the same thickness as the glass vanity tops directly above them.

Facing page: A curved stainless steel tub and a fluid ceiling shape provide a foil to the room's predominant linear shapes. The designer avoided an overt use of stainless steel, which would have created a cold atmosphere for the bathroom.

and slate samples on a workboard.

By process of addition and elimination, the designer arrived at a material palette that meshed tonally, texturally and in terms of warmth.

"The predominating Babinga African hardwood veneer has a pomele grain, which provides a warm, rich finish," says the architect. "This balances the coolness of the glass vanity tops, stainless steel sinks and tub, and the dark slate floors."

Texture was also important. The Babinga veneer's smooth, furniture-like texture is contrasted by the use of a coarse wood for the ceiling above the tub. Hundreds of geometric micro tiles on the shower stall walls are offset by the irregular-shaped river pebbles embedded in grout on the shower floor.

"The pebbles have a fantastic feeling underfoot – almost like a foot massage, and at the same time provide a safe, non-slip surface," says Gleysteen.

As with the customized windows, proportions were important to the finished effect. The cabinetry handles were chosen, in part, because they could be cut to length. This enabled the designer to select specific handle lengths to play off the proportions of the cabinetry doors. Their slender diameter also matches the thickness of the glass countertops.

The emphasis on straight lines, with the handles, cabinetry and tilework, is also in contrast with the wood ceiling, which has a curved, fluid shape, dipping from the windows and flowing upwards above the shower stall.

Scale was another important aspect of the room's delicate balance.

"The micro tiles are set off against the large slate floor tiles," says Gleysteen. "Glass blocks echo their shape in another size again and provide a translucent screen for the water closet, separating it from the rest of the room."

Architect: Principal in charge: Marcus Gleysteen, AIA, BSA, Gleysteen Design LLC (Cambridge, MA); project architect: Amy Semmes, AIA; project manager: Yossi Zinger

Main contractor: Bensley Construction

Bathtub and basin: Stainless steel corner tub from Diamond Spas

Vanity and cabinetry: Babinga wood veneer oiled with clear lacquer from Kenyon Woodworking

Cabinetry handles: Häfele, in stainless steel

Faucets: Wall-mounted, polished chrome Hastings and Vola from Monique's Bath Supply

Hot water system: Wiesman Gas Furnace Unit

Shower fittings: Grohe and Hansgrohe from Monique's Bath Supply

Shower stall: Custom tiled with granite bench

Floor: Cleft slate tile, in Silver Blue, from Stone Source

Tiles: Iridescent mosaics, in Mint and Fern Green, from Water and Fire

Lighting: Prandina and Fontana Arte from Chimera Lighting Design

Ventilation: Krueger Air Grilles, in stainless steel

Windows: Custom made from Hope's Windows

Ceiling: Fir tongue-and-groove paneling, with clear finish

Glass blocks: Delora

Photography by Sam Gray

Enlightenment

This light-filled bathroom is the result of blending two small, dark spaces, and paying close attention to surface detail

Left: This bathroom was the result of the marriage of two smaller spaces. Interior designer Meryl Hare, of Hare & Klein, has created a light-filled room with a feeling of an opulent retreat.

Below: Black marble bowls provide a counterpoint to the Italian limestone vanity beneath.

A room's ambiance can be attributed to several diverse factors – from the light flow to the surface finishes. Find the right combination, and the room's desired character is easily unlocked.

The requirement for the bathroom on these pages was to create a private, light-filled, contemplative space. Initially, the floor plan comprised a toilet area and a separate, smaller bathroom. Both rooms had featured wood interiors and, as such, were dark and somewhat uninviting, says interior designer Meryl Hare.

"Combining these two spaces and introducing light-toned, texture-rich surfaces produced an open and serene environment," she says. "Commanding views and a private outlook contributed to the bathroom's feeling of retreat. The private aspect of the room also allowed for the use of semi-sheer drapes, which helps to maximize the room's natural light."

The designer furthered this feeling by introducing a hand-waxed limestone vanity and hand-waxed stucco treatments on the walls.

"These finishes bring a reflective

Below: The emphasis on waxed limestone and stucco finishes in this bathroom is an extension of the textural focus of the adjacent bedroom and the rest of the house.

Right: A small plinth at the head of the bath provides a seat for a statue of Buddha, and also gives a limited amount of privacy for bathers.

quality and add a sense of depth to the surfaces," says Hare.

The limestone cabinetry was imported in pre-cut pieces from Italy and has a rustic, undulating quality to it, in keeping with the hand finishes.

Centrally locating the bathtub added to the room's feeling of spaciousness.

"Not having to place the bath hard against a wall implies a sense of spacial extravagance, particularly from within the tub," the designer says.

Interior designer: Meryl Hare, FDIA, Hare & Klein Interior Design

Vanity cabinetry: Queensland Walnut

Window treatments: Fittings: Ulf Moritz; fabric: Sacho Hesslein

Bathtub: Englefield Milano by Kohler

Basin: Nero Marquina bowls

Faucets and accessories: Vola

Flooring: Walnut Stone

Tiles: Dolomya Travertine, Bisazza Glass Mosaics

Lighting: Carmen

Photography by Simon Kenny

Natural selection

Chameleon-like, these marble tiles blend seamlessly with the surrounding trees, creating a sense of the forest inside

Left: Architect Warren Hedgpeth used Indian marble in this bathroom to form a connection with the groves of trees that surround the house.

Below: Locally milled Douglas fir, used for the window frames, provides a further visual link to the outdoors.

Opening up a room with large doors and windows is one way to create a physical link with the outdoors. Another way to form a connection is visually — by choosing materials with colors and textures that emulate those of nature.

Creating a strong link with nature was the primary aim of architect Warren Hedgpeth when he designed this bathroom for his parents' home.

"The idea was to embrace the organic nature of the site, with its redwood and incense cedar groves," he says.

"Instead of using urban materials that sometimes become dated, I wanted to use natural materials that would endure."

The search for natural materials led Hedgpeth to select Indian Rainforest marble tiles. It was lines of quartz, as well as the distinctive greens and browns, so reminiscent of tree branches, that drew his attention to the tiles.

"That coloration from quartz is only present in three tiles from a box of ten.

Architect: Warren Hedgpeth, AIA, Hedgpeth Architects (Santa Rosa, CA)

Interior designer: Warren Hedgpeth

Builder: Tavis Construction

Bathtub: Ultra from Bain

Vanity: Piazzo Custom Cabinets

Basin: Conical Bell White from Kohler

Faucets: Purist Chrome from Kohler

Hot water system: Lennox

Shower fittings: Atrio from Grohe

Flooring: Spanish marble from Premier Marble and Tile

Wallcoverings: Benjamin Moore paint

Tiles: Indian Rainforest marble from Premier Marble and Tile

Lighting: Bruck candle from Contrast

Accessories: Baldwin Pulls from Hardware for Doors

Window treatments: Douglas fir from Sierra Pacific Windows

Photography by Tim Maloney

Above: The frameless glass shower stall allows unimpeded views.

Above right: The white conical basins provide a visual counterpoint to the extreme patterns of the marble.

Facing page: The large vanity mirror, which covers most of the upper half of one wall, visually doubles the size of the bathroom.

This spreads out the tones when the tiles are laid," he says.

"The intense coloring of the tiles meant the flooring needed to be more neutral to give the room balance," he says.

Spanish marble tiles were chosen to create a serene atmosphere, counteracting the green and brown hue of the marble.

"The Indian marble is quite intense," says Hedgpeth. "So if it was also on the floor, it would be too much. The cinnamon brown of the Spanish tiles has a levelling effect similar to pine needles on the forest floor. As in a forest, it's the vertical that is the most dazzling spectacle."

Two large rectangular windows, framed by locally milled Douglas fir, exhibit the outdoors to bathers, and accentuate the natural connection. A red fir door is another visual link to the outdoors.

Room to grow

Judicious choice of materials for three bedroom suites in this family home ensures individual bathrooms have enduring appeal

Left: The dark-stained cherry wood vanity in this master bathroom provides a visual counterpoint to the light-filled interior.

Below: Large bay windows and a tall ceiling echo the woodland environment in which this family home is set. The natural surroundings are further reflected in the soft green-painted walls and wooden venetian blinds.

As the bathroom is such an intimate area of the home, it's an opportunity to create a personal interior reflecting an individual's taste and lifestyle. However, in a children's bathroom, there is a need to ensure that the design is flexible enough to change as the child grows.

Interior designer Bill Cook created three bathrooms for a couple and their children. By using luxury materials, such as cherry wood, marble and limestone for the basic elements of each design, the rooms were given enduring foundations.

"In the master bathroom, there is a subtle mix of light and shade, reflecting the homeowner's desire for a sleek, modern interior that is enriched by luxurious touches," says the designer.

In their bathroom, the homeowners requested a clean, uncluttered interior that wasn't aggressively minimal.

Natural light floods the bathroom through a skylight above the shower enclosure and a row of clerestory windows. Limestone on the floors, bath and shower surrounds reflects the light, contributing to a clean, spacious interior.

Providing a visual counterpoint are wide horizontal stripes of dark marble that run the length of the bath. There are also dark marble strips across the shower wall, and dark marble floor tiles are diagonally placed to provide visual accents.

"The result is a master bathroom that

has a spa-like luxury, without being antiseptic," says Cook.

A dark-stained wooden vanity is built into an alcove. This echoes the bay window that houses the bath on the opposite side of the room.

"Cherry wood was chosen for the vanity because of its straight, clean grain. This adds warmth and prettiness to the design," says Cook.

Simple light sconces cast a soft glow across the room, blending with the recessed halogens above the vanity – a lighting combination that ensures shadows aren't cast across the vanity mirror.

Wood Venetian blinds in the bay windows match the horizontal dark marble lines. This provides a visual foil to the room's high ceilings, which dictate a predominantly vertical composition.

Facing page: Materials in this young boys' bathroom were chosen to match the fishing and hunting theme of the bedroom interior next door. The green and brown color scheme is reminiscent of a lodge or cabin. This is reinforced by the decoy beside the bathtub. The wallpaper, that features Beatrix Potter characters, can be easily changed when the boys outgrow children's stories.

Left: This bathroom interior pays homage to the Arts and Crafts movement. The light sconces, window and mirror frames, and tiles are inspired by antique materials and fittings.

Below: A distinctive feature of this bathroom is the accent tiles, depicting small woodland creatures and insects, such as frogs and dragonflies.

It is the sloping angles of the roof in the sons' bathroom which helped inspire a theme influenced by the Arts and Crafts architectural movement.

Tobacco-green colored tiles of varying shades create a mosaic effect on the floor, walls and vanity countertop. A series of character tiles are used both randomly as decorative borders. These tiles depict woodland creatures and are closely modeled on antique tiles.

Interior designer: Bill Cook, IIDA, Vermilion Designs (Atlanta, GA)

Builder: Raymond Smith

Jacuzzi: From Jason

Vanity: Emperador marble, built by Raymond Smith

Cabinetry: Gary Steffler

Basins, faucets and shower fittings: Kohler from Apex

Shower stall fabrication: Raymond Smith

Flooring: French limestone and Emperador marble

Wallcoverings: Boys' bathroom: Beatrix Potter Folia Designs; Girl's bathroom: cloud wallpaper by F Schumacher

Boys' and girl's bathroom tiles: Renaissance Tile & Bath

Toilets: Kohler from Apex

Lighting: Master bathroom: Flos highlighters, fan and overhead light from G2; Boys' bathroom: sconces from Arroyo; Girl's bathroom: mirror lighting from George Kovacs, sconces from Artemide

Window treatments: Wood blinds from Hunter Douglas

Girl's bathroom shower curtain: Calico Corners

Photography by John Umberger

These pages: Triangular-shaped flags above the bath and window suggest a nautical theme. The evocation of the ocean and sky contributes to the room's airy ambiance. Fairy tale motifs on the shower curtain match those found on the armoire in the bedroom.

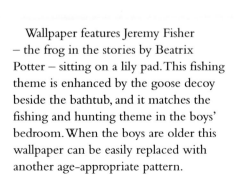

Wallpaper features Jeremy Fisher – the frog in the stories by Beatrix Potter – sitting on a lily pad. This fishing theme is enhanced by the goose decoy beside the bathtub, and it matches the fishing and hunting theme in the boys' bedroom. When the boys are older this wallpaper can be easily replaced with another age-appropriate pattern.

Vintage Americana complements traditional English motifs, with the addition of a brightly colored floor rug featuring American pennies.

Opposite the boys' suite, their little sister has a blue-and-white bathroom, crowned with wallpaper depicting billowing clouds on the ceiling.

Again, Cook was careful not to shorten the lifespan of the bathroom's interior by creating a strictly juvenile theme.

White-painted cabinetry and doors provide a neutral background, enlarging the sense of space for an open and airy interior. The blue-and-white scheme ensures this bathroom is suitable for either boys or girls. Just a few feminine touches – such as the shower curtain featuring a fairy tale motif – indicate the age and gender of the occupant.

"Using accessories which can be easily replaced, ensures that the room will change as the child grows," says Cook.

Shimmer and shine

Mosaic tiles reflect the light in seemingly infinite ways, creating drama and shadowplay in this bathroom

Architects: Colin Leuschke and Andrew Craig from Leuschke Group Architects

Shower stall: Frameless glass

Hot water systems: Rheem

Flooring: Statuario Venata porcelain tiles

Toilet and bidet: Duravit

Lighting: Delta Light

Photography by Kallan MacLeod

Facing page: The fully adjustable blinds above this vanity let in natural light from the adjacent bedroom.

Left: The floor tiles are separated by stainless steel strips. The metallic shine of the strips is replicated in aluminum details, such as the elongated shower head and heated towel rail.

Below: When the bathroom door is wide open, it conceals the bidet and toilet from general view.

Although it might be one of the smallest rooms in the home, the guest bathroom needn't be the most humble. Adding a little sparkle to the decor can transform the room, making it appear a much larger and lighter space.

This apartment bathroom is used by the owners' teenage children and overnight guests. To give the bathroom its own special character, architect Andrew Craig of Leuschke Group Architects selected glass mosaic tiles for the walls, shower and countertop.

"Each tiny glass tile projects the light in a different way to create the illusion of a multifaceted interior," he says.

Halogen lights are strategically placed to enhance the patterns made by the mosaics.

A large mirror above the twin basins and glass shelving adds to a sense of space, belying the fact that at 12ft x 6ft, this is a small room.

The mirror and glass shelving are also a feature of the master suite, and the large porcelain floor tiles continue throughout the apartment.

"This bathroom has its own distinctive features, yet it fits into the overall design of the apartment. Continuity was a key consideration," Craig says.

Index

People

A

Acorn Kitchens   23
Advance Project Team   66
Alan Boyd Inc   131
Albanese, John   118
Alexander Construction   152
Anne Lippincott Interiors   12
Anthony Catalfano Interiors   85
Ascher, Suzanne   42, 45
Asmus, Marc   30-33

B

Barker, Rob   161
Battle Associates   106-109
Battle, John   106-109
Behr Design Studio   138-143
Behr, Josh   138-143
Bieldt, Leon   94-97
Boctor, Mariana   132-137
Boyd, Alan   129, 131
Bradley, Nestor   53
Brandton, Brad   163
Broberg, Erica   26-29, 120-121
Brooks, Kelly   115
Bulthaup   72-73, 85

C

Calaf, Juan   137
Charles R Stinson Architects   162-163
Chatfield, Phil   161
Cheng Design   54-59
Classical Studio   23
Conklin, Elizabeth   115
Conti, Jim   115
Cook, Bill   182-187
Coté, Judi   18-23
Cronin, Morgan   68-71

D

Davis, Kelly   34-39
Design Construction Concepts   142
Dilger/Gibson   118
Dixon, Craig   8-13
Draw The Line Studio   94-97
Dzign   93

E

Edwin Hamilton Stoneworks   155
Erica Broberg Architect   26-29, 120-121
Erskine, John   137

F

Fleur De Lis Interior Design   122-127
Focal Kitchens   98-103
Fontiveros, Jose   132-137
Fu Tung Cheng   54-59

G

Giuntoli, Julian   53
Gleysteen Design, LLC   172
Gleysteen, Marcus   168-173
Grace, David   23
Graham, Michael   80-85
Gramann, Ben   137
Grant, Allison   53
Greenberg, Kathleen   137

H

Hallberg, Renee LeJeune   14-17
HammerSmith   144-147
Harrison Design Associates   116-119
Harrison, William   116-119
Hassell, Rehn   30-33
Hazard, Stasia   85
Hedgpeth Architects   178-181
Hedgpeth, Warren   178-181
Hyland, Christopher   53

J

J Roberts Inc   118

K

KAA Architects   40-45
Katz Studios   109
Kay Kollar Design   152
Kennedy, Debbie   115
Kenyon Woodworking   172
Kinghorn, Bob   38
Kirkpatrick, Grant   40-45
Koolloos, Steve   49
Krekow Jennings   115
Krumpen Woodworks   85
Küche+Cucina Handcrafted Cabinetry   24-25

L

Lanier, Sue   148-153
Leong Yinghow   64-67
Leuschke Group Architects   188-189
Liederbach, Philip   128-131
Lifespace   32
Lin, Amir J   24-25
Lubowicki Lanier Architecture   148-153
Lundin, Richard C   14-17
Lunney, Peter   127

M

Malakoff, Peter   59
Marmig Custom Cabinets   137
Marmol Radziner and Associates   156-157
Marsh Cashman Koolloos Architects   46-49
Matthews Studio   50-53
Matthews, Nestor   50-53
McCary, Mary   38
McClelland, Eric   122-127
McFarlane, Shirley   18-23
Menn, Michael   138-143
Monckton Fyfe   60-63
Monckton, Peter   60-63
Montemurro, John   76-79
Murakami Design   127

N

Nelson, Jenny   144-147
Nolan, Mark   155

O

Olson Sundberg Kundig Allen Architects
Olson, Jim   110-115
Ostrom, Barbara   24-25

P

Pak, DJ   53
Peter David Studios   115

Poticha, Andy   138-143
Pranich & Associates   131
Pritchett, Todd   8-13

R

Radziner, Ron   156-157
Roberts, Jim   118
Rothman, Eric   144-147
Ryan Associates   53

S

Sala Architects   34-39
Schneider, Marshall   154-155
Scott, Kathy   154-155
SEA Design   45
Semmes, Amy   172
Shubin + Donaldson Architects   90-93
Shubin, Russell   90-93
Sintesi Design   132-137
Skyline Design Group   12
Smith River Kitchens   29
Smith, Amanda   89
Smith, Raymond   186
Stanley, Nancy   152
Steenstra, Erica   137
Steffler, Gary   186
Steven Cabinets   38
Stevenson, Ron   158-161
Stinson, Charles R   162-163
Stone Interiors   155
Stone, Stacy   155
Streeter & Associates   163
Streeter, Donald   163
Stringfellow, Susan   150-153
Sueki, Sachiko   137

T

Tejeras, Miguel   137
Todd Pritchett Design Studio   8-13
Tosdevin, Chris   72-73
Tow Francis Architecture   164-167
Tow, Thomas   164-167

V

Van Winkle, Kyle   109
Venegas, Maria   137
Vermilion Designs   182-187

W

Walker Warner Architects   154-155
Walker, Brooks   154-155
Weeder, Erica   131
William Beson Interior Design   14-17
Wilson, Dane Robert   53

Y

Yunker Associates Architecture   30-33

Z

Zampolin & Associates   24-25
Zeff, Andrew   93
Zinger, Yossi   172

3 Studios   14-17

Products

A

AEG   70
AGL Glass Specialties   137
Aktiva   118
Alinea   115
All American Floors   93
Alno   75
Amana   79
American Appliances   137
American Standard   146, 152
Andersen Windows and Doors   16,121
Ann Sacks   23, 38, 59
Antique Designs   23
Apex Supply Co   118, 146, 186
Aquastar   155
Architectonics   59
Arroyo   186
Artemide   186
Asko   32, 89
Atrio   180

B

Bain   180
Baldwin Brass   180
Barbara Wilson   45
Benjamin Moore Paints   16, 180
Berlin Food Equipment Co   59
Besselink   131
Best   53
Bilecky Brothers   38
Bisazza   157
Bisazza Glass Mosaics   176
Blanco   12, 38, 85
Blatka Paneva   23
Bodenschatz   166
Borma   63
Bosch   12, 23, 38
Broan   142
Bruck   180
Bulthaup   85, 72-73

C

C Lighting   23
Cadet   152
CaesarStone   133, 137
Calico Corners   186
California Art Tile   157
Capri   152
Carmen   176
Cherokee Floors   146
Chicago Faucets   131
Chimera Lighting Design   172
Christopher Hyland   53
Concinnity   146, 157
Contrast   180
Corian   61, 63, 99, 103
Country Floors   93
Craft Art   23
Custom Rock International   38

D

Dacor   53, 85
Damar Stone   142
Daniel Otto Painting   163
DeDietrich   66
Delora   172
Delta Light   189

Diamond Spas   115, 172
Dogpaw Design   115
Dolomya Travertine   176
Donghia Fabrics   142
Dornbracht   115, 137, 157
Dulux   49, 79
Duravit   189

E

Elkay   45
Englefield Milano   176
Etoile   109
Eureka   127
Eurolite   127
Eurostone Concepts   152
Excel Homes   16
Ezequiel Plumbing   137

F

F Schumacher   186
Falcon   97
Fire   152
Fisher & Paykel   38, 49, 66, 70, 89
Flos   109, 186
Fontana Arte   172
Fordham Marble   85
Fox Marble   53
Franke   25

G

G2   186
Gaggenau   59, 73, 79, 85, 89, 100, 103
Galaxy Gas Products   155
GE   12 , 38, 29, 59
Genesis   55, 127
Geocrete   59
George Kovacs   186
Georgia Lighting   118, 146
Greenheck   85
Grohe   16, 53, 59, 66, 142, 172, 180

H

Häfele   97, 172
Hansgrohe   172
Hardware for Doors   180
Harrington Brass   32
Hastings   172
Herbeau   25
Hettich Innotech   70
Holly Hunt   163
Home Expo   121
Hopes Windows   172
Hunter Douglas   186

I

Icona Draperies   93
Ideal Standard   97
Illuminations   146
Ilve   70
In-Sink-Erator   70
Interior Dynamics   142
Iris   38
Iron Works Tellieur   163
Islero Design   32

J

Jason   186
Jenn-Air   103

JS Hardwood   137
Juno   137, 142
Jura   97

K

Kenmore   70, 97
Kenyon Woodworking   172
KitchenAid   25, 45, 85
Kohler   16, 109, 115, 118, 121, 131, 137, 142, 161, 163, 176, 180, 186
Kolkka Tables   23
Kraft   29
Kravet Fabrics   142
Krumpen Woodworkers   85
Krueger Air Grilles   172
KWC   38

L

La Cornue   85
Laufen   166
LBL   146
Le Grand Palais   85
Lee Jofa   53
Legacy Company   115
Lehman Hardware   155
Lennox   180
Liebherr   103
Lightolier   109
Loewen   38
Loom   59
Lucarini   53

M

Marble Creations   118
Marmig Custom Cabinets   137
Marvin Windows   32
Masonite   134-135
Master Custom Doors & Windows   137
Maytag   29
Mecho Shades   115
Metalmorphosis   152
Miele   45, 49, 59, 73, 85
Mister Steam   142
Monarch   118
Mondoluce   49
Montis   66

N

Natural Stone   146
Nero Marquina   176
Nutone   121
Nu-Trend Cabinet Co   142

P

Panasonic   70, 146
Paris Ceramics   85
Paul Decorative   118
Pedalworks   85
Peerless Rug   142
Pella Windows   29, 142
Picture Line   75
Plexiglas   125-126
Plyboo   58-59
Poggenpohl   75
Prandina   172
Pratt and Larson   93
Premier Marble and Tile   180
Pulp Studio Glass   137

Q

Qasair   49, 63, 89

R

Real Goods   155
Renaissance Guild   16
Renaissance Tile & Bath   186
Rheem   189
Richelieu   127
Ricketson   109
Rinnai   49
Rocky Mountain Hardware   155
Rohl   12, 23, 25
Rosieres   89

S

Sacho Hesslein   176
School House   45
Seiho   32
Sharp   97
Siemens   66
Sierra Pacific Windows   180
Smeg   49, 63
Smith & Fong   59
Sonoma Tilemaker   45
Sonya's Place   38
Speakman   152
Starline   97
Stickley Furniture Co   93
Stone Source   172
Stone Tile   127
Studio Steel   23
Suburban Electric   163
Sub-Zero   16, 23, 25, 29, 32, 38, 45, 53, 73, 85, 97
Sumi Glass   142

T

Targetti   79
Tech Lighting   59
The Winhall Collection   23
Thermador   12, 23, 38, 53
Tile by Design   16
Tiles Plus   163
Toto   142
Traditions in Tile   23
Traulsen   85

U

Ulf Moritz   176
Ultra   180
Urban Developments   155

V

Van Anderson   163
Veneto Glass Tiles   142
Vent-A-Hood   16, 23, 59
Vetter Stone   32
Viking   16, 25, 29, 32, 45, 91, 93
Vitricolor 20   157
Vogt Plumbing   163
Vola   142, 152, 172, 176

W

Walker Zanger   12, 137
Water and Fire   172
Waterworks   59, 85, 109, 131
Wiesman   172
Wolf   38

TRENDS
where ideas take shape

Print, TV and Web

Trends Subscriptions
Trendsideas.com

LIKE WHAT YOU SEE?
THEN SUBSCRIBE TO THE TRENDS SERIES

Ten magazines a year offering fresh ideas in architecture and interior design – delivered straight to your doorstep. Your subscription includes two editions each of Home & Architectural Trends, Home & Living Trends, Kitchen Trends, Bathroom Trends and Remodeling Trends.

Extensive photography, informed editorial, and the latest in products and services ensure you are up to date with what's happening in home design.

Subscribe to Trends now, and we'll send you 10 issues for only $83, delivered within the United States

Go online to subscribe at the Trends website:
www.trendsideas.com/us/shop